ANDRE HAYKAL JR

What They Won't Teach You

How Young Entrepreneurs Can Find Success OUTSIDE of The Classroom

This book is dedicated to my dad, who believed in me enough to support my dreams and ventures.

And to my mom, for loving me for who I am and encouraging me to follow my passions.

And to Roger, for pushing me to live up to my full potential.

Contents

Acknowledgement

I want to thank my parents for making it incredibly easy for me to become an entrepreneur.

I am beyond blessed that my parents have supported me in everything that I have ever pursued, no matter what anybody else thought. Entrepreneurship is not the norm, and it is also not always cheap (you can ask my dad about that one yourself). Entrepreneurship at a young age is rare without the support and guidance of parents like the ones that I was blessed with.

This book would have never been possible without my parents, even though I wrote it all myself (I promise!). They allowed me to pursue my wildest dreams, and instead of doubting me, criticizing me, or holding me back, they supported me and guided me along the way.

Roger has been an incredible mentor to me, and he pushed me to be better and to work harder and to do more. He showed me that I am capable of greatness, no matter what anyone else says.

I hope that with the future success of this book, my parents will become an example for other parents out there who may be raising a dreamer and entrepreneur like myself.

If you are a parent and you are reading this book, I just want to genuinely say thank you. I also want to challenge you to allow your kids to fully embrace who they are so that they can pursue their dreams without limits.

I also want to thank my amazing editors, Sam Rich and Nicolas Gregoris. You guys were such a big help! Lastly, I wanted to thank my launch team: Roger Brooks, Christian Bonnier, Colton Emmett, Imran Battla, Jordan Gross, Kishan Patel, Satvik Sethi, Brandon Gaydorus, Arooba Najaf, Jake Pierson, and Leighton Blackwood!

What People Are Saying

"I am extremely impressed with the amount of tactical value you can get out of this book. Andre is someone who will undoubtedly make an impact on this world." - Tyler Jack Harris

"Andre is the real deal! He is truly IGNITING the next gen of young entrepreneurs with his work." - John Lee Dumas

"What They Won't Teach You does a great job of bridging the gap between education and first-hand entrepreneurial experience. It's a great guide for any young entrepreneur looking to set themselves up for success." - Dave Meltzer

"Andre is 19 but yet has the mind of a 45-year-old. It's incredible to see that today's youth has individuals like him leading his peers to a better future. His podcast Real Talk University and his book are refreshing takes at helping to bring more awareness towards the idea that true education doesn't end with school, but rather just begins. I highly recommend his book to anyone who needs a reminder that we have one life and we must

make it count." - *Pejman Ghadimi*

"I'm very impressed by Andre, to say the least. At 19 his mindset is where most people aren't in their 30's or even 40's. While in school he's already thinking outside the box and absorbing so much knowledge that is not taught in school. I can't wait to see where he will be in five years!" - *Eric Damier*

"In What They Won't Teach You, Andre puts self-education in the spotlight, leading the way for young entrepreneurs to achieve more OUTSIDE of the classroom." - *Nathan Chan*

"What They Won't Teach You is an amazing achievement by a young man who demonstrates that true learning and success comes from defying the conventional norm. As my mentor once said 'While you were at school, I was out learning!' Andre is the epitome of courage, action and a story that will inspire you to greatness!" - *Peter Sage*

Be sure to leave a review on the Amazon product page after reading this book. This will help Andre tremendously. Thank you all so much for your continued love and support.

Why, How and What

Why

My name is Andre Haykal Jr, and at the time I am writing this, I am 19 years old. I know what you're thinking, what 19 year old wants to write a book? What does an inexperienced teenager have to offer? To be honest, I said the same exact thing before starting my podcast, Real Talk University. Like my current situation writing this book, I had absolutely no idea what I was doing, a complete shot in the dark. Turns out, I was able to make an impact on hundreds of high school and college students with ambitions and dreams as I had. I am writing this book for that same purpose - to make an impact on students who want more out of life; students who stand out in unique ways other than high grades and great attendance, students who don't feel the need to be the most popular kid in school, and most importantly, this book is written for students who do not yet realize their true potential. I wholeheartedly believe that this book will allow you to find and live up to your true potential.

But why am I doing this? You must be wondering why a first-year college student with loads of school work, a successful business podcast, a business venture startup, and of course, familial responsibilities, decided to add writing a book to that monstrous mountain of work. I have a lot to share and writing this book will not only help students like myself, but it will help me as well. It will help me get to know myself better. It will help me to build better habits and be more disciplined. It will give me credibility in the business world. But most importantly, it will allow me to take another step closer towards becoming the best version of myself. I can only hope that it will do the same for you.

How

When I first made my decision to write this book, I had absolutely no idea how to go about it. I thought you had to have years of experience, knowledge, and practice. I never once thought about writing a book in my teenage years, but in 2019, I promised myself that I would do anything and everything to elevate myself and my life. I had no idea what I signed up for because a few days later, one of my mentors approached me and told me I had to write a book. It was the same mentor who had told me I had to start a podcast, so I figured he knew what he was talking about. Following his advice, I made the commitment to publishing my first book before I turn 20.

I included this section in the book for the readers who want to write a book themselves but don't know how or simply do not believe that they are capable of doing it, because I was in that same position. The best advice you'll hear is to simply get started. You may be left shaking your head, asking "but Andre, where? How? Are you crazy? I couldn't possibly do that!". Take a minute. Breathe. It's going to be okay, YOU can do this.

The best way to get started is to determine what you want to write about. Ask yourself, "What am I passionate about? What do I want to share with the world?". After you've got that part figured out, you will need to determine how long your book will be. A good length for your first book is typically around 150-200 pages. Next, you'll need to organize your thoughts. To do this, simply write down 10 key topics relating to what your book is going to be about. These will simply be your chapters, and by doing the quick math, you will know that each chapter should be 15-20 pages. You now have the content organized and a better understanding of how you want your book to look. The next step is simple, but it is the most important. Just start writing! We will talk about the process in more detail later on in the book.

What

Well, if you made it this far, thank you. This is the part where I tell you what exactly you will be reading and learning about in the remainder of this book. When I was first approached about writing a book, this was the topic that I was most uncertain about. I could not really come up with an idea or topic to write about. But, I found a topic that I know will be worth both reading and studying.

This book has one goal - to help you to become the best version of yourself. The way I will try to help you do this is by teaching you what they don't teach you. Of course, 'they' refers to schools and universities. Let's face it, they can't teach you EVERYTHING. My lawyer insisted I include the following disclaimer: I have NOTHING against going to school or doing well in school. I have a strong academic background and have been in school for over 13 years now. We will touch more on this later in the book.

But think about it like this. If we brought back someone from the dead who was alive in the 1800s or early 1900s, he/she would be absolutely mesmerized by modern society. They'd be amazed by the planes in the sky, the vast amount of cars, and most especially, digital technology with things like televisions and smartphones. The world has advanced at such a rapid rate since their time with new technology and innovation. But if that same person were to walk into a classroom at the local high school or university, it would most likely feel very familiar to he/she. The point is, the education system has not caught up. It is not up to date with modern society, and so we need alternatives.

I want to help you guys have success inside and outside of the classroom. If you can be successful in both places, why not? Why not push yourself to be better all around and to max out your life? Once again, I have nothing against high school or college. But I have met a lot of great people through my experience in education. With that, I also have had a lot of great mentors; such as great teachers (well, that probably only applies to Mrs. Howard). We will touch more on the importance of friends and mentors later.

I just KNOW without a doubt, that there is a major shift happening. College is not as important as it was years ago. Education can be found elsewhere, for much cheaper. College education in the US is grossly overpriced, so I want to equip the next generation so that they have all of the information and resources that they need to succeed in the real world.

Now that we've got that controversial topic out of the way,

what is this book *really* about? I have organized this book into eight key chapters that entail components and qualities that I have used to get the most out of my education, time outside of school, and life in general. I believe that by equipping yourself with the knowledge and tactics shared in this book, you will be able to achieve your goals faster. You will also learn of ways to start an online business, or a side hustle, like the one I created during my last two years of high school. You will learn to use the time you have, not only outside of school but also the unrealized time you have during the school day to work on your goals and dreams. I want you to consider some questions before you start this book. Ask yourself the following as you are reading:

"What do I want to get out of this book?"
"What areas of school am I struggling with the most?"
"What do I want to work on outside of the classroom?"
"How will I apply these topics to my everyday life?"
"How can these tactics help me to achieve my goals faster?"
"How can these tips and tricks create more time for myself?"

Always be asking yourself how you can apply what you read in this book to your own life. That will be the biggest component in getting the most out of this book. Now there is only one more question to answer before you decide if you are really going to read this book:

"Hey, Andre, who is this book is meant for?"

This is meant for anyone who is searching for more in their life; for anyone who is looking to make the most out of their time, and for those who not only want to discover the best version of themselves but also learn how they can fulfill that version of themselves. Also, this book has some specifics towards students. Specifically, high school and college students because that is the only area of life I have experienced thus far. But I also know this, *everyone* is a student. Always. There is so much knowledge available. Even the wealthiest men and women in the world of all ages are educating themselves constantly through books and other resources. If you accept the fact that you are *always* a student, then this book will help you tremendously. I hope you enjoy!

Goals

Write down your goals. What do you hope to get out of this book? Consider measurable things like GPA, income, weight, TV time, etc. Make it personal to you, it can be anything!

Chapter 1: Establishing The Right Mindset

————————————————————————————

"Once your mindset changes, everything on the outside will change along with it." - Steve Maraboli

————————————————————————————

Step 1: Believing In Yourself

The most important quality of being successful and setting yourself up for success starts with believing in yourself. Radically changing and improving your wellbeing or lifestyle all starts within. The first thing people ask me about having success is "how do you do it? Tell me how to get rich, show me what to do." But in reality, there is no step by step path to success. But, I can tell you that the number one most important and crucial quality you must have is believing in yourself. I'm not talking about just believing in yourself, I am talking about what I call "believing out loud". Take a minute to think to yourself:

"How can I show others that I believe in myself?"

1

"Why should others believe in me?"
"How can I invest in myself?"

By asking yourself these questions, you are making your worth clear to yourself. Nobody will invest in you or into your company if you aren't prepared to invest in yourself! So, by "believing out loud", you are constantly investing in yourself in front of peers, family, business partners, etc. How? Simple. There are tons of ways to do this. For example, read books more often. This shows that you are dedicated to educating yourself and becoming the best version of you. Another example is investing real dollars and real-time into something you are working on, such as a company or startup. When you go out, ask investors for their funds. How the hell do you expect them to confidently invest in you when you haven't put any money or time into it yourself?

There are also other ways that you'll need to "believe out loud" so that you can get to where you want to be. First of all, you have to mentally accept what you are working for and what it will do for you. You have to truly believe that you are worthy and that you deserve what you are asking for. A lot of people struggle with believing they deserve this change or these positive things to take place in their life. But, you have to believe you deserve it! You are good and you are worthy. If you do not truly think you deserve what you are working towards, then work harder! Show people that you deserve it. Outwork everyone around you. That mindset will shift to you knowing that you are worthy because you work your ass off.

Having self-confidence is huge. I'm going to be straight up with you, you'll face some mentally draining challengers. You'll face betrayal, doubt, and other lows of your life. This is called paying the "success tax." How do I know this? From an interview I did with Alex Morton on my podcast. In the episode, Alex explained how success has its own demons at all the different levels you reach and the way to prepare yourself is to accept them and "fail forward".

This is the reason that you have to first start with your mindset. Once you have the self-confidence you need to get started, you will need to make a shift. You will need to shift all your beliefs, goals, and confidence to your heart. You have to make this shift so that no matter the failures, the adversity, the doubt, or the betrayal, you will never give up on what you know you deserve. You will not be able to rent headspace to anyone if those beliefs are still floating around in there, so move them to your heart now.

One of the best ways to do this is through gratitude. Start every day thinking about things to be grateful for. You have to realize that you were chosen to be put on this earth. You won the race, you are 1/400,000 that made it on to this earth and you get to play the game of life. Be grateful! Your ancestors worked their whole lives to have an opportunity like we have here today to create magic and to leave a legacy. So, before you get started working towards your dreams, you must be confident in yourself to be able to make those dreams a reality. If you are ready, we will move to setting your goals properly.

Step 2: Setting Goals

You've probably heard this a million times, but it is absolutely pivotal to your success. Setting goals is so important, I can not stress this enough. Goals have changed my life in a huge way. For years, I would hear all these successful people talk about the importance of not only setting goals, but also reading them out loud and writing them down. It never really occurred to me that I needed to start doing this. When I didn't have any goals, I would sleep in. Feeling unmotivated and tired, I wouldn't have any inspiration in the morning to wake up and get things done. But as soon as I began to set goals, things changed rather quickly. I first set ten important goals that I hoped to achieve in the year 2019 and I wrote them all down on a whiteboard so that I would see them multiple times on a daily basis. We will cover the process of how exactly you should set your goals in just a second here.

One of my goals read "I will write and publish my first book before December 2nd, 2019." Under this goal, I included steps on how I would get there, one of them being that I would set my alarm for 6 AM (two hours earlier than the time I would usually wake up at) so that I can write for a good two hours straight with no distractions. So, as I began to do this, I was shocked at the way I felt every morning waking up and getting two hours less sleep than usual. I felt energized, inspired, and motivated to get out of bed. This is 100% because of goal setting. The goal I set for myself required actionable steps, and waking up at 6AM to write was one of those steps towards achieving my goal. So everytime I would wake up, I knew EXACTLY why I was waking up, and what I needed to accomplish because of this. If it wasn't for goal setting, this book would almost certainly not exist.

So, what is the best way to set your goals? As I said, so many of the greatest life coaches and leaders preach the importance of setting goals. But, there are different strategies to doing so. What worked for me was starting with why, which I adopted from Simon Sinek. So, when you are setting your first goal, first ask yourself why you want to achieve that goal. Here is an example of what *my* WHY looked like when writing this book: "To increase student awareness of opportunities outside of the classroom and enhance their ability to become the best version of themselves."

Once you have a clear and motive driven why, then you can move on to your WHAT. This is where you will write a cut throat sentence on what exactly you will accomplish and when. It is imperative that you set a goal that can be measurable. It is also important to set an exact day you wish to accomplish this goal by. The most important part of this sentence is starting off with the phrase "I will..." because it breeds self confidence. Another great thing to think about when setting your goals is to live as if you already possess them. Make your "I will..." statement clear enough so that you can paint a picture of it in your mind, as if you have already achieved that goal. Do this on a daily basis and your mind will go to work to achieve it. Here is an example of what my WHAT looked like when writing this book:

"I will write and publish a bestselling book by December 2nd, 2019."

The last step of setting your goals is to write down actionable steps on how you can get to the finish line. What will be required to accomplish your goal? This includes things you can do on a daily basis, ideas that you will explore, deals that have to get done, investments that have to be made, and so on. These are essentially what I call "micro goals." They are mini goals and tasks that will enable you to accomplish your bigger, more concrete goals. Here is an example of what my HOW looked like when writing this book:

I will wake up at 6AM every day to write for one hour.

I will write at least one page per day.
I will review and edit my writing daily.
I will submit my book to editors for their opinion.

The most important thing here was just writing on a daily basis. I needed a system where I would pump out at least a page a day, so that I would have a decent length book written by July. This changed everything. This was only one of my ten goals. This helped me to understand what I had to get done on a daily basis. Rather than waking up feeling uninspired and not really knowing what I should work on and why. Setting goals made me 100% aware every single day of what needed to get done and setting daily goals is also super important. As I said, these can be seen as "micro goals" as well. You can set daily tasks that will ensure you are working towards accomplishing your bigger goals. But, the most important thing is that you are taking action on this. Again, as I said earlier, I would read and listen to all the greats, including people like Tony Robbins, Gary Vaynerchuk, Grant Cardone, Ed Mylett, preach the importance of doing this exercise. But I never realized the power and importance of actually going out and doing this exercise until I did it myself, and it shifted the direction of my life. So, before you go any further, I want you to write down your goals right now. At the end of this chapter, I have provided you a space to do so. So, before you continue reading, write down three important goals for you. Flip to the end of the chapter and start plugging away. Go through the steps we just talked about. Divide it into three sections titled why, how, and what. Once you have these written down, we will continue to work towards making these dreams become a reality. But, don't forget to paint that picture in your mind of you already possessing those goals.

One thing that we have to touch on before diving into the next chapter is how this will play out. If you think by achieving these goals, you will be happier, then you already lost. The key is to be happy now. Rather than depend on the achievement of these goals to bring happiness, you have to be in a happy state prior. You have to be in a position where win or lose, you are still happy. Too often, entrepreneurs will rely on numbers and goals and end results to bring them happiness and the life they think they deserve. In reality, they already had all of that, but they were never in the state of happiness before that. Being happy is easy. Don't over complicate it. Just think happy thoughts and you will be happy. But more importantly, by achieving these goals, you will be fulfilled. So make sure that before you start working on these goals, you have to be happy and you have to work towards being fulfilled through your goals.

Step 3: Thinking Positive

In this section, we will talk about the importance of thinking positive thoughts. Again, all of these steps go hand in hand, so make sure you are following along and taking the appropriate steps and actions to establishing the right mindset. The first thing that you must understand is that life happens FOR you, not TO you. What do I mean by this? This essentially means that life isn't so much about what happens, but more about what you do about these things that happen. It is your choice on how to see life. What is your perception of life? You can choose to see events in a different light.

A good friend of mine, Peter Sage, really showed me the power of having a positive mindset when approaching any situation in life. When we had him on our podcast, Real Talk University, he told us about the time he went to maximum security prison for a financial crime that he did no wrong in. You'll definitely want to check out that episode. Rather than being fearful, he was excited. He saw this as an opportunity for him to share his message and his teachings to people who didn't have access to these things because they were locked up. In his own words, rather than going in as a prisoner or a criminal, he went in there as a "secret agent of change". How badass is that?!

Through that experience, Peter won many awards, prevented many suicides, and even wrote a book about what was going on while he was there, titled The Inside Track. He had a great way to describe this situation and it applies to all uncomfortable situations in life. He says "Your environment doesn't define you, it gives you the opportunity to define yourself. But if you have no ability to handle uncertainty, and you think the river of life should go straight, then you're in dismay land. Every river bends, you have to learn how to sail with the bends rather than resist them or try to swim upstream.".

Another thing I have to mention is to not be in the reactionary state of mind. You should be anticipating and expecting things in life to happen for you so that you have a plan or steps to execute on after this does happen for you. So, right now, I want you to drop the whole spiel about how all of these bad things have happened to you, because everything that has happened in your life has happened for you in some way. Whatever higher power you believe in, I will use God for the sake of my own beliefs, you have to understand that they have bigger dreams and a path set for you that you can not yet see the full version of. This is what makes it the most challenging, is not being able to see what the master plan is. You just need to have a little bit of faith!

So, back to the positive mindset. Positivity is so much more powerful than you might think. If you are always seeking out the positive rather than the negative, than your energy levels and happiness levels will rise rapidly. Rather than enduring life, enjoy it! By thinking positive and always seeking out the good rather than the bad, your mind will start to filter out situations and scenarios that in the past, were detrimental to your life or mental health. Positive thoughts attract more positive thoughts and more positive happenings in the physical realm and the same thing goes for negative thoughts, so it's your choice after all!

Now, how does one always think positive? There are many routines, both when you wake up and before you go to bed which will prime your mind to think and manifest these positive thoughts for you throughout the day. One great exercise that you can try is setting your phone away for the first hour of everyday. Rather than checking emails, text messages, sports outcomes, etc, set your phone away so that your mindset and day is not influenced by a negative result that you may have come across on your phone. Another great thing to practice is the Tony Robbins morning priming routine. If you are unfamiliar with Tony, Robbins, pause this book and go check him out right now. He is what I call the "Godfather" of all entrepreneurs and successful life coaches that are around today.

His routine is very very simple. All you have to do is ask yourself a set of seven questions when you wake up everyday and three questions before you go to bed every night. I've read this before many times, but again, like goal setting, it took me a longer time than it should have to actually start doing it. So in the morning, you will ask yourself these seven questions:

1. What am I happy about in my life right now? What about that makes me happy? How does that make me feel?
2. What am I excited about in my life right now? What about that makes me excited? How does that make me feel?
3. What am I proud about in my life right now? What about that makes me proud? How does that make me feel?
4. What am I grateful about in my life right now? What about that makes me grateful? How does that make me feel?
5. What am I enjoying in my life right now? What about that do I enjoy? How does that make me feel?
6. What am I committed to in my life right now? What about that makes me committed? How does that make me feel?
7. Who do I love? Who loves me? What about that makes me loving? How does that make me feel?

Make sure that you write these down in a notepad or on your phone so that you remember them and eventually make this routine a habit or instinct when waking up. I was amazed on the change this brought upon me. I started to wake up earlier, but with more motivation and energy to get myself out of bed. Another neat thing about this is that it forces you to seek out these questions throughout the day, knowing that you'll need some answers for when you ask yourself that next morning. So, by thinking these questions to yourself throughout the day, you will constantly be seeking for happiness, excitement, something to be proud of, something to be grateful for, something to be excited about, and so on. And it will almost instantly change your life and your level of happiness. So, last but not least, here are the three questions to ask yourself before you go to bed every night:

1. What have I given today?

2. What did I learn today?
3. How has today added to the quality of my life?

Again, very simple, but also very effective. By asking yourself these questions, it allows you to self examine your day and see what you did good, bad, etc. It also allows you to self reflect on some happenings from that day to see if you learned anything that really made an impact or change on your life. The last question adds value to everyday. It simply forces you to find value in everyday, no matter what has happened that day, because every day will contribute to our self growth or to our pursuit of happiness.

So, I want you to give these a try. The change they have had on my own life has been tremendous, and I'd love for it to do the same for you guys. But most importantly, remember to think positive. Rid yourself of negative thoughts. Life doesn't happen to you, it happens for you. So, get on with it and get to work on yourself!

Step 4: Controlling Your Thoughts

Do you ever think about the questions you ask yourself sub-consciously? What are you curious about? What are you trying to solve? What kind of questions are you asking yourself and why? Understanding and controlling these thoughts can be a powerful way to manifest what you want in your life. For me personally, I have always thought different than most people. I am always questioning my surroundings, being hyper alert and curious of what is around me and why.

I think the reason for this is because I have very high set goals, and they are always on my mind. Because I am always thinking

about them, I am always observing my surroundings and apply-
ing their relevance to the pursuit of my goals. By obsessively
thinking about achieving these goals, your subconscious mind
will open up a new space in your mind, which will then trigger
your brain to go and work to fill that void. Once your brain
opens up that space, your subconscious mind will start to pick
up and focus in on your surroundings. You'll begin to notice
things you've never noticed before. All of the sudden, the right
tools and the right people will present themselves to you.

Another method to practice that will enable your subconscious mind to go to work for you is through affirmation
statements. These are similar to your goals, and can be written
in the same journal or notepad as them. Simply take the time to
write down a handful of affirmation statements. I have provided
spaces at the end of this chapter for you to write down a few
of these statements that you come up with and to help you
organize your thoughts. To help you get an idea of what they
should look and sound like, here are a few of mine that I had
written down before writing this book:

"I am so grateful that I am a best selling author."
"I am so grateful that I am the host of the #1 business podcast."
"I am so grateful that I earned seven figures in 2019."
"I am so grateful that I have mastered social media."

Notice how every statement starts with the phrase "I am so
grateful..." This is important because you have to replace fear
and hope with gratitude. Always be grateful, and also tell
yourself that you will be grateful when you achieve these goals
and when these affirmations become reality. These are just a
handful of the statements I used to write out for myself. By

telling yourself that you are grateful for things that you do not yet have may sound crazy. But, it absolutely works. By telling yourself you already have something that you don't yet have physically, your subconscious mind will go to work to make that become a reality. Your thoughts will simply become a physical reality if you take immediate actions to work towards their fulfillment. We can't sustain the images of our goals and reasons without the belief that we can truly achieve them. So, this all relates back to the main idea of the chapter and believing in yourself, because the rest of this book will not be effective and beneficial for you if you do not have the right mindset going into it.

Step 5: Quick Disclaimers

Let me just set the record straight, anyone who has picked up a copy of this book can achieve greatness. You don't have to have the best grades and the highest test scores. You don't need to have perfect attendance. You don't need to be rich, or come from the best family. You don't have to be a certain age. You don't need to have a certain amount of experience in business. Most importantly, you don't have to be the popular kid. Later in the book, we are going to talk about your friendships, and how to be a leader amongst a group of friends who might not think the way you do. But let us get this straight, you are already amazing. You are awesome! Believe that. You are one of a kind, you are unique, so do not feel the need to conform. Be you. Be who you were born to be. Everyone is different, and everyone is awkward, nerdy, and weird in the light of others. But, that is what makes us who we are and more importantly, that is what makes us great. You already won the day you were born, so go out and have fun. Don't take life so serious!

Whether you know everything about business or absolutely nothing about business, it does not matter. I was very young when I started working on personal development. A younger age than most people, but it can be very beneficial to follow my path. The most important thing is not to be mislead. You can't let anyone tell you that you aren't capable, because again, you control your own thoughts; and by doing so, you can manifest anything that you truly want.

You will only manifest what you think you deserve. You get out of life exactly what you *think* you deserve, and nothing more. This is why the activities we went through so far are vital. You can read all the business books out there, all the textbooks in school, and watch all the YouTube videos. But, nothing will change until your mindset changes. You have to truly believe that you deserve what you want out of life. Most importantly, do not let anyone ever tell you or convince you that you don't deserve things.

Step 6: Realizing The Opportunities

The world is changing rapidly everyday, with the advancement of technology having such a massive impact on all of our lives and the way we do things. What you must understand is now is the golden era for people like us. Anyone with an iPhone and a brain can start an online business. Anyone with drive and ambition can actually take that business and make a living out of it. We are so blessed and fortunate to be living in a time like this, where we can be instantly connected to mentors, teachers, coaches, and so on at the tap of a button. There are opportunities everywhere.

One of the most common excuses I hear from people is that they don't know what they can do, or how they can add value. Some of them think of ideas like starting a podcast, starting a social media agency, then automatically discredit themselves. They tell themselves that they couldn't ever make something out of doing that because someone else is already doing it. Well, ask yourself, are the companies that are providing those services meeting every need and solving every problem of every potential customer out there? No chance! They might be cashing in on maybe .001% of the potential business. There is opportunity for everyone, and there is way more than enough success to go around.

If you have a smartphone, than that gives you access to trillions of opportunities to make money or create value for the world. Get rid of all the excuses that you have been making up in your head. You have to do that now, or else you will never achieve greatness. None of the greats or wealthy businessmen made excuses. They took extreme ownership, meaning they accepted the fact that everything that happens is a result of their actions. Everything that happens in life happens for them, not to them.

At the time I am writing this, there are so many new ways to create value in the business world online. Trending ideas are things like podcasting, wholesale real estate, social media marketing agencies and social media branding in general, affiliate marketing, dropshipping, flipping, and so many more things. You just have to go out there and look. Find one of these things that you can work passionately on. Find a unique way you can approach the market and start working on that idea.

Another major excuse or reason that people don't get started is because of lack of capital. 99% of the opportunity out there doesn't require thousands and thousands of dollars like a lot of people think. Instead, it is more about your own time investment. The money isn't always needed up front, and even if it is, there are resources out there to help you go and get it. You just have to be aware and open your eyes a little more so that you can see them and take advantage of them.

Another crazy thing is social media in general. There is so much hate and talk about its negative effects, but the opportunity it gives you is remarkable. You can build a funnel of customers directly through social media, something that was never possible. We will talk more about social media as a double edged sword later on.

There is opportunity everywhere, and the number one step to taking full advantage is to become more aware of it. In the future, this opportunity might not be around or in a surplus like it is today. We have to be grateful for it, and at the same time, do everything we can to take advantage of it. Another huge thing is if you are still in school as a student, there are even *more* opportunities for you. Access to these opportunities are even easier because of the resources around you. Being a school student, you will have access to state facilities, things like local incubators and think tanks. You will also get help and attention from local leaders, who will be astonished by your goals, ambitions, and the way you thin. This will open up doors for you to get the funding and the direct mentorship you need.

For myself, being in college has been a blessing in disguise. Because I am a college student, I have full access to facilities like our local incubator. I am able to participate in things like the accelerator program, which gives me access to state of the art facilities and resources to help me get my business launched. But, it has also helped me tremendously with my podcast, Real

Talk University. Right off the start, we were able to get tons of high level guests on our show for interviews. By sending them interview requests using our school emails, they see that we are still in school. By doing so, they are more willing to participate in an interview on a young hustlers podcast.

The opportunity is out there. At this point, you should fully be aware of it. As long as you have established the mindset we talked about so far, you will be fully equipped for success. You are now one step closer to becoming the best version of yourself. But, there is one last thing to cover before we go into the remainder of the book; taking the next step and taking action.

Step 7: Start Now

The most important element of this book is tying together everything you learn with one thing, and that is ACTION. You must take immediate action. You can not sit and ponder your thoughts, waiting for the right time to take that next step. No, you have to step up now. The time is now. Because every single day you wait, the journey and the road to get where you want gets that much tougher and that much longer. The odds will continue to stack up against you the longer you wait.

So yes, you need to start now. You have read the first chapter up until this point and I have equipped your mind with the tools you need. You are now able to take massive daily action towards success. I know from personal experience that action is the most vital quality to becoming successful. All too often, people will shy away from starting, because they don't believe in themselves or their ideas. I used to doubt myself. I used to be fearful of the end result, so I never started. But over the years,

I have learned everything that I have talked about so far and everything that we will talk about later on. Everything I have learned thus far has changed my life in so many ways.

If you are hesitant to start now because of fear of failure, you need to check yourself real quick. The most important state, is to being happy. Think happy thoughts. Be grateful, show gratitude. Lead with love, not fear or hate. You have to understand that you will fail at times. Life will knock you off your feet but, if your mindset is in the right place, then the result isn't so important. Life is just a game. Be grateful that we get to pursue what we want. Enjoy the journey, get back on your feet and try again. Everyone fails, but it isn't truly a failure if you learn from it.

So you have everything you need to get started but, what's the first step? Well, it depends on what you want to accomplish. Everyone will have different goals, and that is great. But, you have to decide on a plan to attack those goals. But, don't sit around trying to come up with the perfect plan. In reality, that is just a defense mechanism against getting started. There is no such thing as a perfect plan. Nobody can come up with a foolproof plan for success, and that is the beauty of this all. I can't write a book telling you exactly what you need to do to succeed. But, I can tell you that it all starts with having the right mindset. Accept that you will fail and realize success is never guaranteed. So if you know you will fail, why wait? Why hesitate? Why not start now? Why not fail early on, learn, fail again, and continue to learn? Every failure takes you closer to success and the results you have been longing for.

For myself, I would always try to improve my understanding of things. I wanted to know the ins and outs before getting started. I was hesitant to start things and wasn't sure where it would take me. I would watch Gary Vee, read books, and try to soak up as much knowledge as I could up until the point where I realized that I needed to make a change. I needed to do something that changed the direction of my life, and this was only possible through taking action.

So the story goes, I thought of starting a podcast about something I am very passionate about, which is success outside of the classroom. Essentially, the topic and motivation behind this book as well. So the first thing I did was text my friend Christian who is passionate about things like self-education, financial freedom, and so on. I asked him if he wanted to collaborate and he said yes. To be fully honest with you, we had absolutely no clue what we were doing. We didn't know anything that goes into podcasting. But, we didn't care. We knew that we would learn as we go, and we would pick up a loyal following who'd be able to follow along as we went through the learning curve that led to us getting better and better every single day. We simply got together that same day, and took immediate action by recording and publishing our first episode, rather than waiting and second guessing ourselves.

The easiest way to do something is to just go out and get started. Keep it simple! You don't need all the answers, and you will never get all the answers upfront so stop waiting around for that to happen. Go out and get started. I can not leave you with better advice than just getting started. As my friend David Meltzer would say, enjoy the consistent persistent pursuit of what we call happiness.

My Case Study

This section will be where I take you through my own experience with these steps to give you an idea on how it can be implemented and how I benefited from the steps I share with you. It will be included at the end of every chapter going forward and will serve as a chapter wrap up or summary.

Step 1 was to believe in yourself. I have to admit, as a kid, I was not the most confident. But I did know that I was really good at one thing, something that my peers and classmates had no knowledge on. I gained confidence and started to believe in myself through focusing on my personal development. I would self educate frequently, and I would always invest time outside of school into my business endeavors and passions. I was confident that I would succeed because I was willing to do more.

Step 2 was to set goals. Like I mentioned briefly in that section, I was never the person to set goals. I actually never set goals up until the point of when I started my podcast in late October of 2018. When I started to study goal setting and how to properly do it, things changed dramatically. Things got done faster, we got better faster, and we got to where we wanted to be faster. This book would have never been written if it wasn't for goal setting. My goal was to wake up at 5:30 AM every morning to write for an hour straight with no distractions. This was part of my bigger goal, to finish and publish my book before my birthday in 2019. I would have never achieved these milestones without setting goals.

Step 3 was to think positive. This was one of those steps that you might overlook, but it is extremely vital because it ties in to all the other steps as well. By thinking positive and always trying to find the good in every situation, you can get more done. I was able to find positives while in college, even though I had no desire to be there. Not only was I keeping my parents happy, but I was networking and prospecting the students for my podcast and future endeavors. Your network is your net worth, so start building it now.

Step 4 was controlling your own thoughts. This was something that came naturally for me. But, when I found out its importance, I started to master it. I would always ask questions and be super curious about my surroundings. But, I never knew you could use these thoughts in a powerful way. I also started to practice affirmation statements, and that helped boost confidence and productivity to new heights.

Step 5 was just a little section I put in to show some disclaimers that the readers may have thought of after reading the first four steps. Again, you don't need any prior experience. You don't need capital, I was broke when I started. Most entrepreneurs are broke starting out, what makes you an entrepreneur is going out and changing that.

Step 6 was to realize the opportunities around you. Since I was always interested in these things, realizing the opportunities wasn't quite hard. They were all over. If you develop the mindset we talked about in the first five steps, then the opportunity will present itself to you multiple times daily. Just be ready to accept and act on it. I specifically realized the surplus of opportunity after reading *Crushing It!* by Gary Vaynerchuk.

Step 7, my favorite step, was to just start now. None of the stuff we talked about or will talk about will matter if you aren't willing to take action. For me, action was key to my success. As soon as I knew what I needed to do to get to where I wanted to be, I took action. I started to write this book the day that my mentor, Roger Brooks, suggested me to write it. I started my podcast the day I thought of the idea. Don't wait.

Affirmation Statements

Write down 3 affirmation statements here. Refer to pages 11 and 12 to read more about what they are and how you can create some for yourself. Make sure to read these to yourself daily!

Goals

Write down your goals here using the method and steps we talked about on pages 3-6. Make sure to keep these somewhere safe so that you can read them to yourself daily.

Chapter 2: Cashing In On Your Passion

———————————————————————

"Skills are cheap. Passion is priceless." – Gary Vaynerchuk

———————————————————————

Step 1: Finding Your Passion

The first and most obvious step is to find and understand what your passion is. I know for myself, it was frustrating because I wanted to find my passion so bad but I just couldn't. I knew that if I found something that I was super passionate about, then I would be able to work on turning it into a business. That was exactly the case when I finally found my passion. I always knew two things about myself, I loved entrepreneurship, things like building startups and the whole idea of working for yourself. But, I also loved to share news, and to provide help and tips to my friends and family even if I wasn't an expert. I always wanted to voice my opinion.

But, there were also things that I hated to do. I hated public speaking. Back in the day, I was never able to deliver a compelling speech because I had pronunciation issues and more importantly, I didn't think highly of myself as a public speaker. I love communicating, but I hated to actually speak

23

and share my true voice. When I decided to start a podcast with my best friend, I totally forgot how bad my voice sounded. But, for some reason, I didn't even care. This is a perfect example of how one finds their passions. Because as soon as we put out our first episode, I was eager to put out another one. It was just fun for me to do.

I absolutely loved to talk about my passions (entrepreneurship, business, financial freedom) and share them in a way that I was also passionate about. This served as an amazing lesson for me and I think for all people. Your passions and talents are found when you challenge yourself to be uncomfortable, or to feel insecure. I was definitely not comfortable with hundreds of people hearing my voice for an hour at first but, I started to not even care. I did it for self-fulfillment. I found something that made me happy, and the next step was to become the best to ever do it.

From that day, we have grown at an insane rate in terms of listeners and viewership. We have also had the pleasure of interviewing some amazing people that I myself have looked up to for years, people like Grant Cardone, Gary Vee, Tai Lopez, and so many more! I could have never seen myself doing this. I was literally practicing my biggest fear in front of my biggest inspirations and role models, and it was the best feeling ever. My goal is for all of you to find something that makes you feel the same way.

The first thing you have to understand is that none of this is easy. It is not easy to find your passions. Some people find their passions when they are young children; and some people don't find their passions until later in life, when they are in the middle of their career. No matter what the case is for you, that is okay. I was always so eager to find mine as soon as humanly possible.

There is a way to search for what your passionate about, which will lessen the time it will take you to achieve your goals.

The best way to find your passion is to try everything. More importantly, get uncomfortable. Do anything and everything. Don't limit yourself, because you never know your true self until you find your passion. For a lot of people out there, you can also look for overlaps in your life. Passions don't have to be a general idea or hobby. They can be complex, and it can be a mix of a ton of different ideas and traits.

Another great way to find a passion is to find where you perform at your highest level. Think back to a time in your life where you thought to yourself, "man I crushed that!" What were you doing at that time? How did it make you feel? This is important because your backtracking to a time where you performed at maximum potential. Finding your passion is finding an area of your life where you can perform and later feel amazing.

So once you have found something that has sparked your interest and energy levels, you need to dig deeper. You need to go out there and study this activity or unique passion of yours. Study how your mind and body changes when you are performing that task. Dive deeper and learn of new ways to do this passion of yours. How can you make it unique to yourself? Study it for long periods of time so that you will not only completely understand why it makes you feel the way you do, but also how to become the best at doing it. The only way to cash in with your passions is to stand out and to be unique. Other people will share your passions, but how can you stand out and make those passions be unique to yourself?

Another important thing here is what we just talked about, which is discovering your why. Once you understand why it makes you feel the way you do, than you will master your why. For me, I was passionate about my podcast because it allowed me to share my ideas and messages with college students like myself. It allowed me to educate and add value to the lives of thousands, and at the same time, it allowed me the opportunity to sit across from my life role models to ask questions and spark up an engaging conversation.

So, once you have found your passion, you must do what it takes to make it unique to yourself while also mastering it in every way. You have now found your purpose.

Step 2: Start Your Business

So, you decided that you want to start your business. Once you have found an idea that you are confident in and passionate about, the next step is to give it a go. So let's get into some of the technicians that go into starting your business. If you are still stuck on finding an idea, than stop thinking so hard. You don't have to have a burning passion for whatever business idea you chose to start. Simply find a problem in your life or a noticeable problem in the life of those around you and come up with two things. The first being a solution, and the second being how you can get paid for that solution.

The most important term and strategy that you must be aware of when starting your company and going forward is "bootstrapping". This means that you will spend little to no money on the first version of your product or app or whatever it is that you are building. I made a huge mistake with this when I started my first app, Your Call, and I would hate to see you make the same mistake. I paid a high price to get the first version of the app developed and we ran into a boat load of issues with designers, developers, and many more. The project ended up taking over 12 months to complete and my hands were tied due to the money exposed. We also went out for a trademark way too early, and got caught up in a legal battle for the name that cost us way more funding than we had available. So, whatever you do, please do not make these same mistakes.

By bootstrapping, all you need to do is make an MVP version of your app. No, MVP doesn't stand for what you think it does. MVP stands for Minimum Viable Product. Essentially, this means that you are producing a platform or product that is the least sophisticated but, still has the main functionality and solves the main problem you identify early on. There are tons of resources out there that can help you get this developed or produced in a few days times for free or at a small cost. By the way, bootstrapping doesn't mean that this will cost you nothing. It's the difference of thousands of dollars to hundreds. Again, if you aren't willing to invest a little time and money into yourself, then you picked up the wrong book.

The best way to approach this if your idea is an app or website is to design the layout. Draw some wireframes, which are basically rough sketches of what you want built, and send them to a designer. You can get professional designs done for cheap, and if you don't know where to find people for this, than you can simply reach out to me to do it. Or, just do what I did. I had no idea how to design or do wireframes but, I simply took a day out of my summer to learn how to do it. It will pay off, and this is something you'll need to get into the habit of doing, which is taking the extra step and putting in the extra effort to get to where you want to be.

Whether your idea is a software, app platform, or a physical product or idea, you'll need to find a test group by doing some simple market research. Once you have put together a presentable MVP, you will want to find your ideal audience. Come up with some questions or feedback guidelines for potential customers. Put the MVP in their hands and let them determine if it is something they'd use. Does it fix the problem you set out to solve? Does it include all the necessary features? Is there anything there that doesn't belong? Is the idea clear and easy to follow? Asking a set of questions like these will be key and you'll need to be proactive about doing this. Find 25-50 of your ideal customers and perform this research and record the studies in a spreadsheet or journal of yours.

If your idea is validated by your customers, you now have the go ahead to build this product. There are people out there who will buy and use it. Now, you have to decide how you will capitalize on this. How do you plan to monetize your idea in a way that it will be sustainable and profitable in the coming years?

There are tons of ways to monetize anything. The most basic way is to charge a flat fee that is more than the cost to produce and distribute that one unit. For my app Your Call, I had a similar structure to that of Uber and Lyft. My app connected referees with sports league managers and games that needed their services. The app was totally free to use and download, although we would charge commission fees on the payments sent to referees. You can do something similar to this, where you take a cut out of transactions made through your app. If you are struggling to find a way to monetize your app, feel free to reach out to me or again, be proactive about it and do your own research. I am always willing to advise startups and young students working hard on their ideas and dreams.

Now that you have all of this information settled, you will

need to put together a presentation called a pitch deck. There are thousands of templates on the internet that you can use for this. A pitch deck is simply a short concise powerpoint presentation of what your business concept is. It usually includes the problem, the solution, the MVP product, the ideal customer, monetization strategies, and growth plans. You'll be able to get a better idea of this by doing a simple Google search. The point of this is to present it to investors and business professionals to either find a partner or find funding for your company. You'll be able to find the original decks of companies like Airbnb, Uber, Lyft, and many other startups that were able to raise hundreds of thousands of dollars in funding. Be sure to take your time with this!

Step 3: Proof of Concept

The next step you'll need to take is to prove that your concept works. Prove that it is filling the needs of your targeted market. Prove that your ideal customer is willing to pay x amount of dollars for that void to be filled or that problem to be solved. There are plenty of ways to go out and do this, but the important thing is that you do not skip this step. For me personally, when I started my first company, I procrastinated. I kept pushing this off. But when I realized why I was doing it, than it became a lot easier to prevent that.

The whole psychology behind pushing things like this off, is the fear of failure. I pushed it off for weeks because I was scared that my product and app would not solve the problems of my ideal customers. But, once I changed by mindset, I never held anything off. I changed my mindset to a thinking if my ideas failed to meet expectations, new opportunities would open up for me to work on something new. If I kept procrastinating than I would never have the chance to work on something new.

So, rather than pushing things like this off, go out and try them. Get it done and then analyze your results. One thing you must accept is that over 90% of these startups fail before they are even launched. There is a very high chance you will fail, especially the first time around, but that doesn't matter. Every great entrepreneur has failed and has gotten knocked down over and over. Being a great entrepreneur requires you to be able to handle uncertainty. There is never certainty of failure. You need to change your whole mindset on failure and rejection, because as an entrepreneur, you will fail and be rejected more times than you could ever imagine.

So, back to the proof of concept. A good way to do this is to put a version of the MVP in the hands of ideal customers to get their feedback. It also may be smart to not mention the product at all, but rather leverage your college or high school status. Ask them a set of questions and just tell them that it is for a school research project. This will help you to get more authentic and transparent answers and results regarding the problem and pain points you identified. You will then have to validate your value proposition. Does it meet their needs and is it something of value to them? Are they willing to pay monthly subscription fees? Are they willing to pay commission charges on in app payments?

Your value proposition has to be unique and clear. What are you offering that isn't already being offered? How are you different than their current provider? Or other providers out there? One thing to keep in mind is that there is always a way to do it better. Just because a company is already doing something in your target market, don't give up. Technology and business is changing every single day, so there will always be an opportunity to outdo others in your market.

Now if the results from your market testing and proof of concept case studies turn out in your favor, great! What you will need to do is write up a summary paper along with some numbers and stats from your study. You can add this to your business plan, pitch deck, and other resources that you will curate later on. Another great thing is that you can tap into these people for endorsements or funding. If you tell them that you are bringing a product to the market to fill the pain points you discussed with them, they may be willing to pitch in to make it happen!

Step 4: Trial & Error

The number one mistake students and young entrepreneurs make when they are first starting out is the fact that they quit or give up if the first version of their idea or app doesn't work, or isn't the most needed product. What you will need to learn how to do right away is pivot. This is a term in the startup world that is used and executed by every successful company multiple times. By pivoting, it can mean a lot of different things. It can mean that you are shifting the focus on the problem that your company sets out to solve. It can mean that you developed a new way to solve the original problem. There are endless ways to pivot, and that is why entrepreneurs thrive with pivoting, because they are creative people.

Pivoting was something that I had to learn when working on my second app with my cousins. We worked tirelessly on an app idea that would enable a better and more enjoyable sports betting experience, but there was one problem. It was not yet legal! So, we had to think. What can we pivot to now, that will allow us to focus on that original idea later? Meaning, if we could shift focus to something that we can act on now and it is successful, then we can later use those funds, as well as the connections and the brand established, to build our original app idea quicker and more efficiently. This is exactly what we did. We went through the state to build a version of our app that was legal, and we put our original idea and solution on the back burner for now.

So, don't fall in love with just one idea or just one solution. You will need to go through some trial and error. Nobody gets it perfect the first time around! The easiest way to do this is to know that it is part of the process and to expect it under all circumstances.

Step 5: Bootstrap Now, Raise Funds Later

The most effective long term method for founders to secure funding to launch their startups is through the process of bootstrapping. This allows founders to maintain full control and ownership of their venture without the unwanted pressure and influence of outside investors. In my opinion and from my own personal experience, this is the most important step to fully understand. When you start your company, app, startup or whatever it is that you want to work on, you have to set out to bootstrap. What does that even mean? Bootstrapping is when you use your own funds or your own pool of money to build out the first version of the app. In most cases you only have a hundred to a few hundred dollars to tap into, and that is plenty.

What bootstrapping forces you to do is to learn new skills which you would have previously paid for. It essentially forces you to self educate during your own time to learn a skill set that lets you move closer to your product launch. Bootstrapping is the way to go because it forces founders to adapt to the surrounding challenges quickly through interactions and gradual improvements which, is essential to startup success. Also, because founders who bootstrap have little to no cash on hand, it will push them to release products and updates quicker in efforts to validate the needs and pain points of their customers.

When I first started my app, Your Call, I made this mistake. We set out to hire a design agency to complete a mockup and prototype of the app. I never did app design and was unfamiliar with how to learn or how much it is even supposed to cost. We ended up paying a firm in Washington thousands of dollars to do a 70 page app prototype. This was a huge mistake, one that set me back financially as well as time wise. What I did not understand at the time was the term and the power of bootstrapping for startups.

As an entrepreneur or a founder, it should almost be your natural instinct to think with the bootstrapping mindset no matter what. Why? Well, bootstrapping is unique and applies well to entrepreneurs because it forces them to get creative. It forces them to adapt to what's going on around them. It forces them to think outside the box. It sparks the creative mindset and can often lead to amazing new ideas for your company. It can also lead to great new strategies that will help get you to the product launch day you and your team are working towards. More importantly, it will save you from blowing a large amount of cash early on.

Well, to make matters worse, the designs provided by this firm were dog shit. So now I was in the hole thousands of dollars, and all I got in return was a poorly made wireframe of what I wanted my app to look and run. What made things worse for me, personally, was when I set out to learn app design. In the summer, I dedicated a weekend to watching YouTube videos and using a software called Sketch to learn app design. It was the easiest thing I have learned and it was also extremely valuable. I was then able to designs app ideas that have been floating around in my head for absolutely no cost in a short time frame, as opposed to paying thousands of dollars to outsource it.

This is so important because early on in your startup journey, this little failure or mistake can be the death of you. This can set you back so far or drain your funds out so badly that you'll never make it to product launch. This is why I am highly emphasizing this skill set so that you are aware. The fact that you picked up and are reading this book of mine makes me a whole lot more confident that you're not the one that will make such a mistake.

Again, bootstrapping can apply to any job or money grab early on in your steps to product launch. No matter what, spend as little cash as possible and make sure it is out of your own pocket. Another mistake and time waster is when entrepreneurs have an idea but have done no work for it other than putting together a pitch deck. Then, they go out to venture capital firms and investors to pitch them in an attempt to get outside funding. I hate to break it to you, but nobody is going to pour money in to your company if you, yourself, hasn't even done so yet. This brings us back to a major talking point and theme in this book, which is, investing in yourself. Do you want to be respected and taken seriously when the time comes when you do need outside funding and management? Then you will have to put in the work now.

You need to invest in yourself. Start educating yourself early on, and then move to the specifics. If you need app designs, learn how to do so by watching YouTube tutorials. If you need wireframes or mockups, learn how to effectively put those together on your own. If you need physical product prototypes, treat it like a science fair project and spend as little as possible but, enough to have it make sense. You have no excuse because there is an influx of new opportunities and resources available through technology and the internet for aspiring entrepreneurs like yourself. This helps to finally bring your furnished ideas to life unlike ever before!

Bootstrapping is no easy task. But what you must have to make it work for you is hard work, grit and most importantly, passion for what you are working on or building. That burning passion and desire to get to product launch will help you to push through the early on failures.

Step 6: Applying Your Classes To Your Startup

If you are a student like I am and you are reading this book, than this step here can be extremely valuable for you. First things first, I made this book because of the things that school or higher education in general won't teach you. But, I am still in school. I am still attending college. College and school, in general, may suck, but since we are already there, let's leverage it and take full advantage.

The first thing I want to cover is networking. If you are in college, then you are constantly surrounded by thousands of students about the same age as you. Start to build a network. Join clubs that interest you. You might find like minded individuals at these clubs and in return, these people may end up being your next business partners. The point is to start building a network of people and friends that you can outsource work to. A very important motto that you should start to live by is that your net worth is your network. So, make sure you are constantly being proactive about this in as many ways as possible.

Another thing that college has forced me to do is to become organized. Before college, I was never organized. But when you have to balance between four classes, writing a book, working a part-time job, managing a podcast, and working on two startups, then you are almost forced to become more organized. LOL!

College also provides you with leverage, which is very valuable when you are building a brand or a startup. By being a college student or nonetheless a "student," you are eligible for student discounts on software and other products. But, more importantly, you have leverage over potential investors and business mentors. Their people love college students and are willing to help students more than others. But, you also have leverage over prospecting and market research. When conducting market research, it will be super easy to collect data because you can sell the prospects on taking the time to help by saying it is for a school project or a research project. Immediately, they are willing to help and they leave all their bias at the front door. You now have access to a super lucrative aspect of business, and you are now able to collect real and authentic data from your market and ideal consumers.

Again, I have no desire to be in school. I hate college. I can not stand going. But there is no value in this attitude towards it. If I am there, than I might as well make the very most of it. If I have to be there, then why not take classes that may interest me or may apply to my business or startup. There is no excuse to bypass this method. Any class, if approached with the right mindset, can be applied to your startup or business.

For example, the entry level writing class at my college was based around a research you conducted on one topic. This research was conducted over the entire semester. Students chose research topics such as politics, mental health, and other hot topics. But my research topic centered around *why* startups fail and, it was very suitable for the course. Through this course, by opening up my mind to think bigger and smarter, I was able to get an amazing grade as well as knowledge that was immediately applicable to the things I was working on outside of the classroom.

The key is to just open your mind to bigger and better possibilities. If you are constantly in the mindset of asking yourself how you can apply your classes to your passion, than you will soon start to realize and learn how to leverage your classes.

Another key recommendation is to take technology classes. Whether it be basic courses, coding courses, etc. Make sure to start taking these early on. By learning how the internet works and how to code, you will be able to run a much more effective company. If you could learn how to code, you'll save yourself months of time and thousands of dollars immediately. So even if the class does not peak your interest, you can always think of it like that. You might as well give it a try, you never know if you will absolutely love it or completely hate it.

The last thing here is to try everything. Again, there are tons of classes that are never considered or looked at by new students because they want to take the routine classes that all of their friends are taking. But why do that? Why not try a class like folktale or cinema? The great thing about taking these wildcard courses is that you may find a new or another passion. You never know until you at least try! There is no point in taking the mainstream classes, you'll just be like the rest of them. You need to stand out and to do that, you will need to capitalize on your passion. You can not do that if you don't even know what your passions are in the first place. So, if you are looking and searching for your passions, this can be a great way to get your answers quicker. You just have to try it!

So the key here is to just change your mindset. Open yourself up top bigger and better thinking. Why sit through a class you hate for three or four months without thinking like this? It doesn't help to slack in this area of life if you are already paying so much for it. Because in reality, you will be there anyways, so why not make the most out of it?

Step 7: Get Your Finances In Check

This one sounds pretty simple but some people just don't understand how important this is. When you first start your business, you will have costs and expenses that will need to be covered. Some of those will last longer and can be recurring, for example, promotions and advertisements. You are going to need to pump money into advertisements at first. Nobody knows who you are or what you do so, promoting will be huge for your success.

So, to effectively do this, you will need to be smart about your money. Make sure you got your money right. Whenever you sell a product or make money of any sort, make sure that it goes right back into the business. Get real for a second. You have to understand and accept the fact that you can't pay yourself for the first few months or years, however long it takes for your business to pick up traction. For some people, it might be hard to understand but when you first start a business, you have to act like you are completely broke. You have to identify the needs in your business and allocate your money to those needs.

Finances are so important when you are just starting out. A smart thing to do is to keep an Excel or Google spreadsheet open to track all expenses and revenue. Make sure that you have breathing room! You need to estimate the 3-6-9-12 month estimated costs so that you can prepare properly for the budget needed. By keeping this spreadsheet available and updated, you will have a better idea of where you are at and how much you have to work with.

Ask yourself, how can I start saving money? What am I spending money on now that can stop and wouldn't affect my life? Identify a few things and cut them off. Now. Yeah, that means stop going out every weekend with your friends. You spend way more than you think during that whole process, not including the time wasted. Yeah, it can be fun at times, but every week? Not needed. It won't work for you. Stay dedicated and make a commitment to this. Someone else is out there working those hours and saving those dollars to beat you and do what you are doing but even bigger and better.

The competition out there is real. The barrier to entry nowadays is so low. You're going to need to use every resource you have to optimize efficiency and increase the likelihood of success. It is all in YOUR hand. Nobody else will determine that for you. So, make sure you have your finances in check and start acting like you're broke.

Step 8: The Solopreneur Trap

The last thing that I wanted to cover in this chapter is a trap that a lot of entrepreneurs often fall in and die. The myth is that you don't need a team, that you can do it all on your own. The term for that is to be a solopreneur. It is the most common and biggest mistake that I see made, especially with our generation of millenials and others. After reading what we have covered so far, you probably thought to yourself that being a solopreneur was the best route to take. But, it 1000% is not.

Solopreneurs do not work and they do not last. The number one reason for that is because of burnout, especially in the beginning stages. There is so much work to be done in the beginning and it is just not possible for one person to, not only identify everything that gets done, but also to get all of those things done effectively. Yeah, it might be easier than ever to start a business today, but the fact remains that you can not do it all on your own.

Behind every great entrepreneur, businessman, athlete, etc is a mentor, or a wife, or a business partner, etc. On our interview with Peter Sage, he explained to us how Sir Richard Branson, one of the wealthiest and most known businessmen of our time, was flat out awful at business. But, what he was brilliant at was hiring and working with people who were super intelligent at business. See how that works? There are different roles for everyone, and not just one person can fill all of those roles.

Another thing about being a solopreneur, is the risk of quitting and giving up. There is no accountability if you are all on your own. You can hold yourself accountable only to such an extent. But, having someone there to constantly remind you and keep you in your best form, is key. So, what happens when you experience those setbacks and failures that we discussed earlier? Because I will tell you, it can get very dark and very lonely during those times. It'd be much less worrisome if you were to find yourself a partner to push through these things with.

So, find a partner. Find someone you connect with and shares the same values with. Someone you can be comfortable around for long hours. Someone that you are able to lead, and able to tell them when they make mistakes, and tell them what they need to hear. It is almost like finding a soulmate. LOL. Not really. Don't overthink it. Most people already know who they want as their business partner. Think about it this way, when you are successful and absolutely crushing it, do you want to be by yourself enjoying that? Or have a partner there with you to celebrate with? Simple answer. Find a business partner!

My Case Study

In chapter two, step 1 was to find your passion. For a lot of people, this is hard to do. It was hard for me, especially. After reading Gary Vaynerchuk's book, *Crushing It!*, I was so desperate to go out there and find my passion. Eventually, after a year or so and many trial and errors, I found my passion through my podcast. I connected the two things I loved most, which was teaching and spreading news, and entrepreneurship. The podcast allowed me to spread stories and teachings about entrepreneurs, to entrepreneurs. But, with all passions, this may be short term. But, that is totally fine. New passions will develop and present themselves to you, and you will have to be constantly open to them finding you.

Step 2 was to simply start your business. I started my first business when I was 16. It was called 24HourProxy, LLC. I had this idea for an internet service in the sneaker resell community. I was a reseller and I used computer programs to secure multiple limited edition shoes and clothing. But, you needed to buy these internet items called proxies. You had to buy them for 30 days, but for our use, you only needed them for the duration of the sneaker release event, which was usually less than an hour. So I started 24HourProxy so that you can rent them for 24 hours, which made them cheaper of course. It was a win-win for everyone. Starting the business was easy because I had mentors like my dad and my grandfather, who have started multiple businesses in the past.

Step 3 was to have a proof of concept. When I started Your Call Sports, LLC in 2017, this was one of the most important steps to take. I was building an app where we would essentially be the Uber for connecting sports referees to sporting events and league organizers. After some guidance from the local incubator and their marketing mentors, I had to go out and prove that my concept was needed. I did this by putting together a clickable prototype and then showing it to potential customers and app users. By doing this, I discovered that there was a pain point, but the way I planned to solve it was not the best approach. So, I went back to the drawing board.

Step 4 was trial & error. With all my companies, including the podcast I recently started, the trial & error process played a huge role. The most important thing with this is, having something to trial. So with all my companies, the first thing I would focus on is having a visual for the product I set out to make. From there, you can edit and revise.

Step 5 was to bootstrap and raise funds later. This was the biggest mistake I made. This is also the mistake you need to avoid in order to survive. When I started Your Call Sports, LLC, I dumped money into design agencies, trademarks, and more shit. I wasted money and time upfront for an idea and concept that didn't work yet and needed tweaking. The one thing I avoided was raising funds from outside investors, which could have been brutal if I had done so because the idea and company was a failure early on.

Step 6 was to apply your classes to your startup. This is a great strategy and one that has helped me to not only enjoy school a little more, but also to have some new tactics to apply to my startups. During my first college semester, we had to take a writing class. My research topic for the entire semester was "Why Startups Fail". Because of this class, I was able to research an important topic to me and my startups while also getting work done for one of my major classes.

Step 7 was to get your finances in check. This is super important, and I found out about this later than I would have liked to. I was always a spender but I was forced to save when I started my podcast because of the lack of money I had in my bank account.

Step 8 was to avoid the solopreneur trap. This is a trap that almost everyone falls into from the start. With my first company, I fell into this as well. I was building the website, growing my Twitter, doing customer service, and so many other things while attending school five days a week. Avoid this step by finding a partner. When I started my podcast, I knew I needed a partner. It has been a lot easier and we have been able to get a ton of work done by having a team of two.

Chapter 3: Staying Organized

"Your life is controlled by what you focus on." - Tony Robbins

---

Step 1: Optimizing Your Time

Yeah I get it, I hear it all the time. You are busy! So am I, and so is everyone else. Optimizing your time is so very important for people who are college or high school students and at the same time, entrepreneurs trying to start or run a business. My friends always ask me how I had time to do both, and do both successfully. In high school I made high honor roll every year and finished with a GPA of over 100. I had 32 college credits after graduating high school. I got good grades, but by looking at the time I spent on school compared to my classmates, I surely did not deserve those kind of grades.

But what people don't realize is that you have to optimize your time, not just extend it. Just because Sally studied for the AP Calculus test for three hours last night and I only studied for 30 minutes, doesn't mean Sally knows more and is more prepared. What does Sally do in those three hours? Maybe read the textbook (useless), checks her phone every now and then (useless), takes a snack break (useless), reads some more (useless) and so on. But during my 30 minutes, I don't have to read, or check my phone, or even take a snack break. I simply do. I would do a practice problem or a mock test. See, if you were to optimize your time at all times, than you wouldn't need to read the textbook. You'd already be familiarized with its content by paying attention during the classes leading up to the exam.

Most students struggle in school because they are not present. What do I mean by this? When they are in class, they aren't focused there. They are checking their phones, thinking about the basketball game that's scheduled for later that day, what the weather is like, what the homework is for other classes, etc. They aren't consuming all the time during that class and dedicating it to that specific class. So, when they go to study for an exam, they have to make up for that time.

By living in the moment and in the present, you will capitalize and consume all information needed when it is shared. If you start to lose focus and check out to the outside world, for example social media, than you are not optimizing your time. Think about it, for every minute you spend unfocused in the classroom or elsewhere in life, you will eventually need to revisit that time later on to make up for it. So, why not get it out of the way right now?

Optimizing your time applies to all aspects of life. Some people don't perform well at their job. But why? Because when they are at their job, they aren't focused on the task at hand. They are focused on what they will eat after, or how they are getting to the football game, or what friends they are hanging out with after work, etc. By not living in the moment, they lose focus and their quality of work is dramatically lower. Grades will be lower, work performance will be lower, and revenue from business will be lower.

In high school, everyone always asked me how I was able to find time for school, 2 companies, a part time job, and free time. Well, there are 24 hours in a day. Most people sleep for 8 of them. Most people use the other 8 for sleep. Now you have 8 hours left. What do you do with those 8 remaining hours? That is what you have to ask yourself.

Step 2: How To Study

This section will mostly focus on how to study for high school and college classes, and I understand that not everyone reading this book is still in school. But I do think that these habits and hacks can apply to all areas of life if you were to look at the general concept of them. Also, you must understand that everyone learns DIFFERENTLY. I just wanted to share my routines with you because I am sure you can tailor them to you own habits and preferences and as a result, enhance the overall process of studying.

The goal of studying is to retain and understand a large amount of information in the shortest time possible. In high school, there were always those kids who would read the textbook from front cover to back cover, but that was never me. I wasn't huge on reading. I was always looking for shortcuts or ways to get a general idea of the information I needed to know rather than every detail that they included in the textbook. Why? Because they would never test you on those small details. You are only tested on 10-20% of the information in there, so there was no point in trying to consume 100% just to retain 10-20%. In reality, this made it even harder to do so. For me, I would prefer conceptual learning over memorization. If I could understand what I was studying rather than just reading and studying to memorize, I knew I would be able to answer most of the questions and do well on the exams.

So, rather than reading the textbook, I used the number 1 tool in all of life, which was Google.com. Especially in high school, where the curriculum is so similar across all schools with the regents and AP programs, it was so easy to find study guides and consumable chapter outlines and reviews. Rather than taking home my textbooks, I actually never touched them. Those stayed in my locker the entire year. But what I did was I used Google to find powerpoint slides or YouTube summary videos on the topics or chapters that I needed to study for. This always worked, especially for AP classes. The important curriculum was highlighted in each chapter on these online resources and rather than reading a 50 page chapter of small printed words, I would watch a 20 minute YouTube chapter summary and take notes.

Taking notes while watching a video was huge for me. It helped me to retain information a million times better than just reading a boring ass textbook. So now, you watch the video once for a full understanding of the concept, and then again to take notes. By the time I was finished, I was done studying after an hour. That is it. There was no need to go the extra step and read the textbook and add more useless information to my brain to confuse myself. And now, I had a few pages of notes from the video that I could use the next morning. Before the test, I would read through those notes a few times just to get a quick refresher. By just glimpsing at some of the words, your brain is able to connect them with the entire concept from the video and the specific details about that word that they talked about in the video. Just a quick disclaimer, this method most likely works best if you are a visual learner.

So, if you use my techniques, what you will see is that you can study effectively in 1/5th the amount of time as before. If you don't believe me, try it out for yourself. The key is to be confident. Just because you study for 3 more hours than I do doesn't mean you are better prepared or that you deserve a better grade than I do. It's the same way in business. You have to find a way to work smarter, not harder. The time you save from these new routines will be vital to your career outside the classroom. You have now freed up a few extra hours every week that you can now dedicate to your startup company. You'll also do better in school, it's a win win!

Step 3: Time Blocking

Now we are going to talk about another great time management skills so that you can get the most out of your days. Since everyone's biggest complaint is about not having enough time, I figured I would focus on some good techniques that you can use to create more time blocks in your days.

First of all, everyone complains about not having enough time, and this is because they let time control them. You have to take control of your own time. There is a great analogy that I like to use after hearing it said so perfectly by a guest on my podcast, Sashin Govender. So, everyday you wake up, $86,400 is deposited into your bank account. As soon as you go to bed, the remaining money that you did not spend that day disappears. You can not get any of it back. When you wake up, your account is reset to have $86,400 in it. If this was reality, wouldn't you be trying to spend every single dollar within that day? Why put any of that money to waste or let it disappear? This is in fact reality. We are blessed with 86,4000 seconds in every day. Since time is money, and I guarantee every single one of you has said or thought that to yourselves before, than why are we always wasting time? If you see time in a new light, than you will start to capitalize and take advantage of the surplus of time that we have in everyday. Because one day, your bank account will not reload.

So, what is time blocking? It is a time hack in my opinion. It is a method that people use to divide up their days so that they are performing at maxout levels and peak states. Just because you are working 24/7 doesn't mean that you are making the most of your time. Say if you follow the same routine every day. What if when you get to 30 minutes of business brainstorming on your calendar, you are worn out or tired from previous activities that day.

Time blocking is a way for you to order the steps in your day so that it is logical to help you achieve max performance. If you are like me and you want to write for the first hour of every day, than that is great, but don't plan to do your calculus homework or business customer service check ups right after. Instead, maybe plan to write Instagram captions or Tweets for the day. This way, you are staying in the writing mindset and reaching peak performance of a writer that day. If you want to read a chapter of a book before you go to bed every night, than it wouldn't be a bad idea to block some time out before and after for studying (reading a textbook) or checking and reading emails.

See, time blocking helps you to organize your day into different categories based on the work you are performing. In the mornings, I like to work on writing things. In the afternoon, I like to work on interactive and high level things such as working out or making sales calls. At night, I like to read things. This makes it so that once I get into one of these levels and phases, I am performing at a high level for each phase of the day since I am focused on that task. If you start to align mix and match tasks, you will start to burn out.

Another great technique is the time you dedicate to each activity. Rather than saying you will study for an hour or write for an hour, why not try these things in 20-30 minute intervals. Chances are, you'll be distracted a handful of times during that hour. But it isn't too hard to get dialed in for a good 20 minutes. Than reward yourself with a 5 minute break or a social media check up. Once you get into these habits, you will feel a change in your workflow mindset. You will shift gears throughout the day and it will feel like a refresher that you had already expected.

Step 4: Beating The Sun Up

Most people wake up around 9 AM or even after that. If I told you that I am more energized, more productive, and less tired by waking up at 5 AM rather than 9 AM, you would think that I am crazy. I am telling you the truth. There is some psychology behind waking up early. Not only do you give yourself another 3-4 hours of time, you will also feel a positive change to your mental state and levels of energy throughout the day.

I used to try to wake up earlier than I usually would because I read books and watched videos of people like Gary Vee and Tony Robbins telling people that waking up early is the key to getting work done, etc. But I could never actually do it. I'd set the alarm for 6 AM and as soon as it went off...SNOOZE. I gave up after trying for a few days, but I later revisited this. When I made the commitment to myself to write this book, I knew that I had to create an hour or so of more time in my day to dedicate to writing. I wasn't the type of person to sleep in to noon or anything like that, and to some of my classmates, getting up at 9 AM every morning was still very early.

But like I said, I needed a time slot to dedicate to this book getting written. So in the new year of 2019, I started to set my alarm to 6 AM. I decided that as soon as I woke up, I would read through the Tony Robbins morning exercise (page 15) and then write on my laptop for a good hour or so. The first day was easy. The next day, even easier. For some reason, I was easily able to wake up early. I couldn't understand why I could wake up easier now but not before. And then I realized. The Tony Robbins exercise was no joke! Well yea sure, it definitely did help me to stay motivated and positive to start the day but there was something else about this whole waking up early thing that I had finally solved. It was solely because I knew what I had to work on as soon as I got up in the morning. Rather than just trying to wake up a few hours earlier every morning to be like Gary Vee, I now had a legit purpose and a why. This was a complete game changer.

Think about it. Why would I wake up 3 hours earlier without any real reason? It made no sense at all. Especially because when you do wake up early, there is an urge to hit the snooze button and to say fuck it, I am going back to bed. But when you make a commitment and dedication to something, everything changes. It is a lot harder to hit that snooze button. Especially because of the way your mindset will change.

When waking up early and going through my morning routine and prayers quickly, I set myself up to be positive and grateful. Then, on top of that, before 7-8 AM even hits, I had completed a major task for the day, which is writing a page or 2 of my books. So, before 8 AM even hits, which is still before most of my siblings and family gets up at, I am feeling accomplished, grateful and ultra positive. On top of that, I enjoy a great breakfast and then I am off to start my day. Even if the day ahead is shitty or slow, I know that I accomplished something great that morning and it makes all the morning.

So, yes, you can do it. You just need to find a purpose. And of course, myself and everyone else still faces those demons telling us to hit the snooze button and wait 10-20 more minutes etc. DO NOT GIVE IN. It might just seem like a 10 minute ad on nap, but scientifically, by doing those things, you will feel more tired the next time you wake up which means you will be less motivated and less productive throughout the day. At least give it a try, because it can be a real game changer in your life like it has been for me.

Step 5: Staying Present

I often struggled with a lot of the advice I have given about time management thus far if you can't already tell. And I think as we get more busy and our calendars fill up more and more, we get even worse with time management. We might be able to complete all of the tasks on our calendar for that day, but does that even matter if we aren't staying present? There is no point in half assing all of those tasks. I would rather crush of them than to half ass them and complete all 5.

This is where time management plays a very important role. When we set our schedule for the day and plan out tasks that we wish to accomplish, we have to stay true to these. The time blocking skill we just talked about will play a huge role in this as well. But if we set a task to write from 6-7 AM every morning, than we have to do exactly that. By staying present, I mean that we have to focus only on what we are doing at the time. If we start to shift focus to the tasks that are a few hours later, than you will be doomed.

By not staying present, there is a whole lot of things that happen that can have a negative impact. If you aren't focused on the task you are currently working on, your output won't be that great. While you are working on that task, you may experience extra stress and anxiety by thinking ahead. This is a huge deficiency in your work and efforts and it can be evidently seen in all work environments. It is great to map out your day and to understand and always be aware of what needs to be done, but if you are supposed to be working on your business plan from 3-4 PM and during that time you are checking answers for your calculus homework, than the results will be poor.

By staying present, we create a sense of focus. I think that a lot of people struggle with time management because of this. They look at what has to be accomplished that day and they get super stressed out and anxious as soon as the days starts. If they are working on their first task of the day, they are typically already thinking about and planning for the last task of that day. And this is a serious problem because it works backwards. By doing this, you are trying to maxout your time but in reality, you are cutting yourself short of what is really available.

Think about it, there are tons of successful businessmen and entrepreneurs who run dozens of companies, have families, obligations, and everything else that we have. Well, they even have the same 24 hours that we all have. This is how they are able to accomplish all of those tasks within a day. If we are just managing school, family life, and trying to start up a business, than we should have plenty of time for this compared to how much these experts are able to accomplish. They are able to do this because they are always present. If they are working on Business B, than they aren't having meetings or checking emails for Business D.

This is also super important to life outside of business. Family life is so critical to your success in so many ways. Having that support team that you can constantly rely on is so huge and will come in handy very often. Like we mentioned earlier, the path we are taking here can be lonely and dark at times, and if it wasn't for my support team aka my family, the odds of me quitting or giving up would have greatly increased. So when you are with your family, stay present with them. Don't be working on or thinking about Business C or the chemistry homework you have to do that night. Stay present with your family and give them your full attention and respect. What ever happened to authentic communications and interactions? Let's bring those back. We can do this by staying present and staying focused on your current task.

Step 6: Plan Ahead of Time

Planning ahead of time is a great way to hack time. So often throughout the day, we are unorganized and unguided in the decisions we make and the actions we take. This can be a major problem because this will most definitely slow you down. A very important law of money and how it works is that speed attracts money. Money goes to where there is speed. You are going to need speed when implementing your plans and taking action on your goals.

This ties in directly with setting goals. Sure, it is a great idea to set massive goals for the year or month etc. But we also need to be setting smaller, daily goals. Daily goals will help us to get to where we want to go, faster than before. Daily wins give us a sense of accomplishment and satisfaction. We can carry this momentum over to the next day and the next day, helping us to move towards our goals with immense speed and determination.

This also helps us to enjoy the process and the journey more. This is so critical because if you aren't enjoying the journey, then you are wasting your time. The journey is the reward, but you won't realize that until you reach the destination that you are aiming for. If you are not enjoying the journey and the everyday challenges and hustle, then chances are you won't last much longer on that path. Why should you? There is no point in doing something that doesn't bring you daily wins and happiness.

Planning ahead of time can be looked at in many different ways. There are tons of different strategies out there, but like everything in this book, the best thing for you to do is to take away the most prominent concepts and make them into your own. Make them into your own, get creative! We are all entrepreneurs, so that shouldn't be too hard.

A great time to plan a day is when your head hits the pillow the night before. At this point, you can analyze your day. What did you accomplish today? What did you fail to accomplish? How did today contribute to the fulfillment of your long term goals? After going through your day, you can now decide what needs to be done tomorrow. It is also not a bad idea to start to journal this. You can stay in bed, just use a note taking app on your phone to log this journal entry daily. From my personal experience, this works best when you set 3 main tasks to accomplish the next day. You can also add a theme to that day. What specific goal are these tasks being implemented for?

Once you have these goals and tasks set for the next day, wake up that morning and before getting out of bed, go over your goals in your head or write them down in your journal. I can not emphasize how powerful it is to write things like this down! Manifestation is 1000% REAL. The last step is simply to hold yourself accountable throughout the day. Take massive action. Goals do not work without immediate actions. This is because of the Law of Diminishing Intent. Every single second that goes by after hearing of or thinking of a goal or path to set way on, you will become less excited and less interested in that thought. This is why it is so important to strike when the iron is hot! You can not afford to waste any time between making these decisions, so taking action is the most important aspect of this concept and of the all the concepts in the entire book. I can not stress that enough.

So remember, part of staying organized in to plan ahead. It is always a good idea to plan ahead for the next day. Start small. Big things can be made small. Build your way up. Celebrate those daily wins. Enjoy the damn journey! Because if all else fails, you will be able to say that you had a great time pursuing your dreams. And you can always start again!

Step 7: Using Resources

It is 2019 everyone, and maybe even a later year at the time you are reading this. The internet is prominent! It will be your very best friend. I will teach you how to take full advantage of the resources out there. Not only that, but I will show you that they exist. The biggest issue is that people don't even know about the resources that are out there, and then if they do, they don't know how to properly use them. I will show you them and then teach you how to use them and leverage them to your full advantage.

The first resource is most likely familiar to everyone on planet earth, but it is surprisingly under leveraged. This is Google Drive. Bookmark that shit ASAP! This will be your home on the internet. This is where your entire life will exist, in the form of files and folders.

So a few things here. Firstly, Google Drive is completely free to use. So you have no excuse at all. Next, Google Drive can be accessed from anywhere on the planet, no matter the device. This means that you can access your files on the toilet in your basement on on the beach in Mexico. Wherever you are, it will be there for you to access 24/7/365. I can not stress the importance of that. Next, you are able to instantly share your files and folders with anyone who has access to the internet, so yea, anyone on the planet. Another great feature of Google Drive is that it is super simple to stay organized. You can create folders for different projects or tasks. If you want to write a book, make a folder for your book and create a new document for each chapter. More on that later. All in all, this should be your go to resource for all things files.

Not to mention, Google Drive also has a Calendar app built in. I know, for a lot of people this is common sense and well known information, but for those who are not aware of how to take full advantage of this, you need to learn ASAP. Google Calendar is a great way to set daily tasks and goals. If you have your Gmail account on your iPhone, than your Google Calendar will sync with your iPhone calendar seamlessly. You can create events that you wish to collaborate on with your friends, and you can even add them to the event by adding their email. If you aren't making use of these features yet, you have to learn how to now.

Don't wait.

Another great resource is Product Hunt. This is my source of daily news. Rather than wasting time reading Twitter or CNN (constant negative news), I scroll through Product Hunt. This is an online directory, similar to the Reddit format, except for the fact that it is a curation of the best new products, every day. It allows you to discover the latest mobile apps, websites, and technology products that everyone's talking about. Later on when you launch your first startup, this will be a great resource for you to promote your own app or website.

Another great resource that I use daily is Todoist. This is a great to-do app that will hold me accountable for my plans and tasks everyday. It is neat because you can get super organized with this tool. You can create separate projects, for instance, I set a project for my book and for my podcast. You are able to add tasks and assign them to different projects, and it will list your to-do list in the order of highest priority in terms of project completion percentage. It is truly simple to use and is preferred over the Reminders app that is standard for iOS users.

A few other resources and tools are things like Trello for agile project management, Slack for team communications, Canva for designs, Basecamp for team collaboration and file sharing, and InShot for video editing. There is a plethora of great resources out there, and I will dedicate a directory in the back of the book with links to all of these websites and more. Just be sure to take full advantage of all of these because they can save you a ton of time and you will become more organized. It pays off later, I promise!

Step 8: Be Obsessed

The last step for this chapter is to be obsessed. Whatever it is that you are doing, you have to be so passionate about it and so obsessed with it that it keeps you up at night. This is essentially organizing your thoughts. Because like we discussed before, thoughts manifest physical reality when backed by daily massive action. It goes back to the quote in the beginning of this chapter:

"Your life is controlled by what you focus on." – Tony Robbins

Read that, and then read it again. We have the power to control what we have and don't have in life. And when you truly understand and believe this phenomenon, your life will permanently be changed.

Look around you. All of those people are your competition. When you aren't focused, and optimizing your time and staying organized, a handful of those people around you are doing those things. Are you seriously going to let them get ahead of you that easily? Without putting up a fight? Being organized and optimizing all situations in your life is key, even when they seem like the smallest, least time consuming decisions. You have to be alert and you have to be organized at all times.

If you aren't absolutely obsessed with what you are working on, than you will get beat. Think about it and be honest with yourself, can you stay motivated doing what you are doing for the next 5 years? How about the next 10 years? Can you handle failure and setbacks or will you give up? If you are even a little iffy about these questions, then find something else to work on. Find something that you can be obsessed about.

There are 4 types of people in business and in life in general.

The first person is that who has no goals. Again, a goal is just a dream but with a deadline or timeline. In other words, a dream but with accountability. Don't be the person with no goals. The next person is that who is goal oriented. These type of people have goals, but they are missing the deadline and the accountability aspect. We talked about how to properly set goals in chapter 2, so make sure that you have a full understanding of how to do that because a goal or a dream is not an effective goal without a deadline. Procrastination will creep back in and create a roadblock between you and your dreams. So, don't be the person with goals but without deadlines. The next person is that of goal mastery. Goal mastery is where you write down your goals. You want to manifest them. You got through the process, you have them set and you write them down. But, like we talk about over and over again, you are not done at that point. Matter in fact, you just got started at that point. You have to get to work! Don't be the person with goals written down but no follow through.

Now, the next person is the person you should strive to be. That person is someone who is goal obsessed. This is where you become what you are working on. You are your business. You have to be your business internally and emotionally. You absolutely must be obsessed with what you are working on. But why? Why is it so important to be obsessed? When you are obsessed, the unexplainable will happen. This is logic. Whatever you focus on tends to grow. When you are obsessed, you are laser focused on your goals and making them happen. And when you start to achieve those goals, it becomes chemical in your brain. Goal achievement produces dopamine in your brain. You will become addicted to success, and that is the goal of this chapter. Get organized in order to get addicted to success.

My Case Study

Step 1 in this chapter was to optimize your time. There are tons of ways to do this, and I have always been the person to make the very most out of my time, especially in school. I am just like everyone else. I hate to study, it is in no way fun. And again, like everyone else, I want to get that out of the way as quick as possible but while also achieving the best results. So, to optimize my time, I stay present. I focus on what I am doing in that split second on time, instead of focusing on what is happening later on in the day. Stay in the moment. Also, studying can be done more simply. Rather than reading entire textbooks, there are people out there who have already did that and made new content that is a fraction of the length with the most important takeaways. That is what you should be studying from, not the textbook.

Step 2 in this chapter was how to study. So like I mentioned, I was always the person to leave my textbooks in my locker from the day we got it to the day we had to hand them back in at the end of the school year. Read a practical business book, not a textbook. Textbooks are fluff, so turn to the internet for resources that can break down the key takeaways from the textbooks. So find a way to work smarter, not harder. I know, I struggle with this all the time too. It is not easy to stay attentive when studying for a biology test. It sucks, so rather than sitting there for 2 hours with continuous distractions, leave your phone in the other room and grind for 30-60 minutes with no distractions. Quality over quantity when it comes to time devoted to studying.

Step 3 in this chapter was time blocking. I sucked at time management before making a commitment to get better at it. That is all this is. I am like everyone else, these are all the things I struggle with, but I am offering some insights on how to potentially improve these areas of your life. Time blocking is a great skill, because it allowed me to devote certain areas of my day to certain tasks and themes. I always sucked at writing. I got terrible grades in writing classes, and I just hated to write. I could never write for more than 20 minutes without getting writers block. But here I am writing a full length book. By devoting an hour of complete focus every morning, I was able to flip the script. Writer's block is not even a thing anymore, it doesn't exist. I beat the sun up, and write for an hour. If I can do it, anyone can. Because I was the worst writer for years.

Step 4 in this chapter was beating the sun up. Again, I was never the person to wake up early and be happy about it. I tried numerous times just because I heard so many successful people talk about it, but time and time again I just could not do it. I figured out why, and it was because I was unmotivated. There was no reason for me to wake up early. When I woke up, I had nothing I wanted to accomplish. So why even wake up early in the first place? That was my mindset, and it is a very common one. But again, you have to flip the switch. Take control. So, the first thing I started to try was gratitude exercises followed by an immensely important task. At 5:30, my alarm goes off, and I go through my gratitude exercise followed by 1 hour of writing for my book. This changed my life forever. My energy levels spiked and my productivity levels spiked. Again, I was never a morning person! But by using these steps, I made the mornings my bitch!

Step 5 in this chapter is to stay present. This is yet again a simple task to practice that greatly helped me recently. I was always the type of person to think ahead, worrying about things that were to come later in the day or week. That took energy and focus off of what I was doing in the present, which overall was a huge loss of efficiency. By staying present, you can ensure complete and maximized efficiency on whatever it is that you are working on. The next step here is what will allow you to do this.

Step 6 in this chapter is to plan ahead. By planning ahead, you are able to stay present. You do not need to be worried about what comes next or the unknown because you are prepared and ready for the expected and the unexpected. Planning ahead was something I would do frequently, but it became 10x more important and critical when I started to take on more responsibilities and tasks, and the same will apply to you guys. So be prepared for when the time comes!

Step 7 was to use resources. I am an internet geek so I was always looking for cool technology and products to enhance my lifestyle and daily routines. They are out there, so you will have to do your own research to test the different resources to see what is the most helpful for you.

Step 8 was to be obsessed. I remember with my first startup, I was never obsessed with what I was doing, but I didn't think it mattered. Unfortunately, I was wrong. When the tough times came along, I was not inspired enough to hold through. But this served as a lesson and it changed the way I do things now. On the other hand, I was always the person to set big goals, but I never wrote them down! I thought that it was all BS and made no difference, but again I was proven wrong. I wrote down a goal saying that I would write a full length book in 10 weeks, and it was manifested. But inside that goal was micro daily goals. And weekly goals. 1 chapter a week was my goal, and by 10 weeks, I had my 10 chapter book completed. Micro goals lead to daily wins lead to crushing your long term goals!

Chapter 4: Become A Leader

"Leadership is not about titles, positions or flowcharts. It is about one life influencing another." – John C. Maxwell

---

Step 1: Define Leadership

People are very mistaken about what qualities good leaders possess, so before we get into how to become a good leader, let's point out some qualities that all leaders have. The number one quality of all leaders is influence. Leaders are able to inspire and impact many people over time. They don't motivate, they inspire. These are 2 very different things. To be motivated is to have a motive for doing something. Motivation is what I call fluff. It is short lived, and doesn't stick with you and it doesn't change you or your identity. Inspiration on the other hand, is a process. Not a moment, a process. It is a process of being mentally stimulated, like a mental spark that pushes you to be the best version of yourself. Inspiration leads to action, and it causes changes in our identity. So, great leaders know how to inspire, not motivate.

Great leaders are also mentally tough in all situations. They are able to keep their cool when things go south. They are able to lead their team, not boss them around. They lead by example. They take ownership of their actions, and they take ownership of the team's performance, good or bad.

In my honest opinion, I do not consider myself to be a great leader. I am young, and I struggle with a lot of these qualities, but everyday, I am trying and trying harder to become a great leader. This being said, I do not have all the answers of what it takes to be a great leader. I know that when I started my first company when I was 14, I was an awful leader. I didn't lead, I gave orders. When I started my next company after that, I still was not a great leader. I struggled to keep my team motivated. I struggled to hold them accountable and to keep them motivated and inspired on what we were working on and why it was important. I struggled to work closely with each one of them to figure out what they would be best off working on. I was too loose, but when I realized this, I jumped to the next extreme and was playing the blame game. Wrong! This is not how to lead, and I have learned this over the years.

After many experiences running businesses and trying to launch successful products and companies, I learned that leadership is so damn crucial to the success of what you are working on. You absolutely have to be a good leader. The nice thing about leadership is that it is everywhere in your life. In sports, in school, in family, in faith, in friendships, in relationships, and in whatever else. It is everywhere! But the great part about this is that once you learn how to be a good leader in one area of your life, you will be able to apply those same principles and leadership skills that you developed to all other areas in your life. It is all the same, and good leaders will tell you that as well. It is common for professional athletes to start successful businesses after their career. Why? Because they are able to apply their leadership skills they learned during their sports career to their business or company.

Leaders are created not born. Everyone has the potential to become a leader. It is in all of us to become a world class leader. But it is up to you to decide if you want to become a leader. Everyone can create influence and value. You just have to be willing to stay disciplined through the process and to stay committed on a daily basis to evolve into the leader you want to become. It is not going to be easy, and it sure as hell is not for everyone. But it will change your life and the impact you have on all of the people around you. So, let's do this!

Step 2: The Process

Like we said, leaders are not born. Nobody is born with the skills and mindset to be a leader. All leaders are created overtime. Leadership is a process, especially to become one. Leaders need to be consistent daily with their actions because teams and people rely on their leaders for decisions and guidance. Guidance, not orders. Remember, leaders are not like a boss. Bosses give orders and are typically not liked by their employees. Leaders influence people to execute on plans and steps. But leaders are everyday people. You and I, we both have what it takes to become a leader, but we must make a commitment to the process.

Leaders are not created overnight. It is like success in business, it does not happen overnight. It may seem like that to the outside world, but there is a lot that goes on behind the scenes. The process to become a leader is through self education, discipline, and hard work.

67

Self education is an important part of the process. Leaders need to be educated on things like the mindset of people. They need to understand how influence works and how they can use it as their top quality. Self education will allow them to learn by example from other leaders. This is by far the most effective way to become a leader. You need guidance and direction to be a leader, and if you aren't willing to seek help from others, than you don't have what it takes in the first place.

The next is discipline. To evolve into a good leader, you need to be disciplined. You need to stay committed to your daily tasks and goals. You need to be on top of your studying habits. Lastly, you need to be a hard worker. If you aren't willing to work hard for yourself, than you won't be willing to work hard for a team of people. Work hard now.

Step 3: Take Ownership

If there is one quality that all leaders must have, it is to take ownership. This was brought to my attention by Jocko Willink, a retired United States Navy SEAL. He is the author of 2 books on leadership, the first beings *Extreme Ownership* and his latest book called *The Dichotomy of Leadership.* These are both incredible books and I highly recommend for your to check them out if you are at all interested in learning leadership skills and lessons from the very best of the best. But for now, I am going to take his concepts and apply them to my audience.

Taking ownership is what good leaders do. This is when you take full responsibility for anything that happens with your team. You are your team. There is no exceptions for this rule at all. This is why leaders lead an bosses boss around. There is a huge difference. We are not here to be bosses or to boss people around. We are here to lead and inspire teams to achieve greatness. If you truly truly truly understand this concept, than you would agree that there is no such thing as a bad team, only a bad leader.

For most of the people out there reading my book, in higher education, we are taught to be the boss. We aren't taught real leadership skills. The popular kids in school aren't leaders, they are more like bosses. They don't inspire anyone, at least for the most part. Leadership is not fully understood at the high school or college level, although it should be. And from my own personal experience, it isn't even in the curriculum. That's just not acceptable. For me personally, I was only able to learn true leadership qualities outside of the classroom through self education. Like I just mentioned Jocko Willink books, among other great ones such as *How To Win Friends And Influence People* by Dale Carnegie. These should be included in the curriculum at all schools. Students need to be exposed to these important lessons and laws of the universe rather than being assigned to read pages of useless textbooks. Textbooks are dead!

So what exactly is taking ownership? Taking ownership is when you come to an agreement with yourself that everything is your responsibility, as long as it has to do with yourself or with your team. There is never anyone to blame, ever. No exceptions at all. You have to take ownership of your actions because they are your results. We can apply this to the high school and college level with a great example here. If you get a bad grade on the test, it is your fault. Not the teachers fault. Not that getting a bad grade is such a big deal, but taking ownership of it is. Don't complain that the teacher didn't prepare you well enough.

You are given the chance to prepare outside of the classroom. What does that say about you as a person? If you are constantly blaming others for your own results. This is such a consistent theme among students in the education system, and they just don't know better. Heck, they aren't even taught these things! But that brings up a great point. If you want to learn to become a great leader, take extreme ownership! Rather than criticizing and ridiculing the teachers and the education system for not teaching me leadership skills, I went out on my own to educate myself on them.

Do not put the blame on others. It is always your fault. You have to own your mistakes and your faults. It is something that so many students struggle with. No matter what, they are always looking for someone to blame.Well, look in the mirror kid! If you want to effectively lead a team, whether it be in sports, academics, business, you have to learn how to take ownership. Good leaders master this skill, and you will too. It just takes discipline and being humble. Take ownership and watch how the outcomes change for the better. This is how you lead, by example.

Step 4: Influence

There is this whole new trend with social media where popular athletes, actors, models, business people, etc are known as influencers. This is great, but it has created and artificial bubble of fake leaders and influencers. Everyone and their mom now thinks that with a few thousand followers, they are an influencer. No! This just isn't true, and in most cases, those thousands of followers that you see are not even real! The influencer marketing spiel has been taken way too far, and it is a poor example of leadership. Unfortunately, it has become more of manipulation than leadership.

True leaders create real influence. They have the super power to create genuine, authentic connections and influence among their teams or groups of people in their niche. Well you are probably thinking, what is their secret? How are they so successful in doing that? This is going to be the most simple and easy advice I will give in this book that you will immediately be able to take and apply to your own life to become the leader you aspire to become. Be yourself. Be authentic. Be yourself. It is that simple, to inspire others and to be a good leader, you just have to be yourself! And luckily enough, being yourself requires no effort at all. By being real and authentic with others, you can create real influence. People are influenced by other people with real and authentic stories, because as humans, we can relate to them.

Think of it like this. Who is more inspiring. Person A is trying to lead and influence by showing his 8 figure bank account, his community Lamborghini, his mansion in the hills, and his nightlife. He wants you to buy his course on how to become rich like him. Person B is like you. He was never the best on the team, and he even got cut from his high school basketball team. He later went on to prove everyone wrong by working his butt off. Who is the more influential person? Well, it isn't person A! It is person B, who turns out to go by the name of Michael Jordan. Person A doesn't have a name, but you can find hundreds of these person A people all over social media. They show off fake bank accounts, they rent a Lamborghini with the other person A people for a day just to take pictures for social media, and they sell a worthless course so that maybe one day, they can actually live that lifestyle that they are showing you they live.

Person A is a prime example of a modern day influencer. The

problem is, these influencers on social media do not create real influence. It is artificial, and it is amped up on market hopium. The consumers hope that by purchasing these courses, they too can have these material goods. They are not influenced, they are amped up on hopium. There is no sense of influence there at all.

Person B on the other hand influenced many many people. Michael Jordan is known to be the best basketball player to ever play the game. His story has the power to truly inspire others. He is just like you and me, he was cut from his high school basketball team! The greatest ever basketball player was cut from his high school team, who would have ever thought?!?!

This is true influence because unlike person A, person B was like us. He represented the rest of us. He was one with the people. Person B was too good for us, we weren't good enough yet. He said that he is nothing like us. How is that inspiring? It is not, that is why Michael Jordan is inspiring and has created such a strong and loyal following because he was like us, and he went on to achieve greatness.

To really have an influence on other people, we have to show people that we are just like them, because we really are. We have to be real with not only others, but also with ourselves!

Step 5: Create Your Own Path

One of the most common themes in the education system is to do everything the way it has always been done. This is just not the way to do things, and more importantly, this is not what leaders do. A great reason why leaders are seen as leaders by others is because they can lead you down a new, creative path. They aren't following the mainstream. They create something different. They stand out.

Leaders are brave because choosing the path less taken can be daunting. But it is absolutely necessary. Leaders are unique and acquire mass followings because they do something great in a different way than everyone else. In school, you are taught what the RIGHT way to do things are. Well, in reality, those ways of doing things are only right to some people, and one of those persons obviously being the teacher. But is there a right way for everyone to do something? Absolutely not. And leaders identify this. They challenge the status quo.

Being different and embracing that quality is huge. In high school, most students are scared to be different. They are scared of being judged, scared of not being liked by everyone, scared of making a fool of themselves, scared of getting a poor grade. In college, students just don't know how to be different. They are there for the same reasons as everyone else on their career or major track. They aren't taught to create their own path early on, so this is only natural for them.

But what happens when you travel down a common path? Why does it matter than everyone in my business school at college wants the same exact thing and is planning on doing the same exact thing to get it? Because not everyone will reach the finish line. Its overcrowded!

Step 6: Be of Service

As leaders in society, we are to be of service to others. It is our duty. We have to be of service to our teams and to our groups. We have to do everything in out power to give them the skills and knowledge to succeed and complete the mission. You must always ask others how you can be of service to them. How can you better their well being? How can you equip them to be more prepared for achieving success? How can you lead them in the right direction without losing their faith and trust in your guidance?

Think about some of the great leaders in your life today. For example, your parents are great leaders in most cases. They truly and deeply care for you, they give you the tools and anything in their power to succeed but they also give you enough room to make your own decisions on what you want to succeed in doing. They are always of service to you!

Think about a boss at work or a bossy teacher. How are thy of service to you, if they are at all? In most cases, they aren't of service. They are the "this is how it has always been done" types of people. And that just leads to "this is how it always turns out" results. This is why in most cases they are disliked and frowned upon by their own employees and others in that organization.

Look around you. Everything you see is made up by humans. Humans like you and I. Why don't people make this more known and emphasized. Everything in life, from material goods to the process and the way things have always been done, was created and established by humans like you and I. Do not conform to the standards set by people that were no smarter than you and I. Be different, and be of service to others. We are all capable of changing the world!

Step 7: Lead Don't Order

This is a common mistake that people make when setting out to be leaders. They try to influence and impact others through force or just being bossy. But good leaders don't do that, they actually lead. There is a great quote by John Maxwell on this, and it goes like this:

> *"If you are a leader, you should never forget that everyone needs encouragement. And everyone who receives it – young or old, successful or less-than-successful, unknown or famous – is changed by it."* – John Maxwell

The biggest misconception of being a leader is that you have to be bossy, in control at all times, and always listened to. But leaders are people who have a team that follow them, and bosses are people who has to push their team to where they want them to go. Would you rather your team to willingly follow you or for you to have to push them?

There are many ways that you can accomplish this influence. First off, when starting a company or working on a startup, hiring employees or finding a business partner is a more important step and sales pitch than anything else in the beginning phases. Having a good team full of people who truly believe in what your startup is working on is so crucial to its success in the long term. I would definitely prioritize this because it is not stressed enough elsewhere.

People talk about the importance of having a solid team but what does that mean? Well think about it this way. How can you know for sure if your employees and business partners truly believe in the company and what you are building? Well, that's easy. You can tell through leadership exercises. Is this team easy to lead? Are they already committed and so believing in what I want to lead them to accomplish that I don't need to tell them much of what to do because they just go out and do it. Or are they always hesitant, slow, lazy, and so on.

Either way, it is all on you. If they are super motivated and truly believe in your mission

as a company, than great, now you have to keep it that way. If not, well you messed up somewhere. When you set out to hire them, they didn't see you as a good leader. You didn't truly sell them on yourself and what you want to accomplish as a company and why they would be an important piece in making that happen. You have to make them feel important! And they are important, because like we talked about before, being a solopreneur is too dangerous. You have to find a business partner, and if you take this very seriously, it can be a huge asset for you.

If you find someone who is willing to do what it takes, understands the job, and doesn't require much direction and coaching, than great, you got very lucky! But in most cases, this is something you will have to practice and a leadership skill that takes time to develop, but the best way to develop this skill is through experience.

You can do a self examination if you already have a business partner so see where you are at as a leader. Ask yourself, do you have to repeatedly ask him/her to do something? Do you have to constantly remind him/her about what it is you are working on and why? Do you feel that you are spending a lot of your time and energy on him/her just to make sure that they are getting the job done? If you are answering yes to some of these questions, than you have to develop better leadership skills.

The best way to lead is by example. Show your employees the passion and efforts that you are willing to put into you business and from that, they will follow your lead.

Step 8: Balance

Leadership can be real tricky at times, especially when you are trying to find a middle ground on different things. Ironically, there is actually cases in which bad leaders exist because they can't find a balance in leadership qualities. For example, you can take too much ownership, and that can cause you to be a lackluster leader. You can hold people way too accountable and hold their hands along the way, and that too is not a good sign of leadership. You can also mentor or work with people to closely and personally which is also another sign of bad leadership. And of course these hold true on the opposite sides of the spectrum, which is more common sense than this side of the spectrum.

Leadership consists of a few main skills and themes, things like being able to lead, being able to focus, being able to be aware and controlling at times, and bring able to take action and execute it properly. But there has to be a balance with all of this.

You need to know when to lead and then also when to fall back and follow other leaders on your team. Yes, leaders also follow. The goal when developing your team in business or in other areas of life is to create more leaders.

By creating leaders down the line, you will be able to share the balance with them. They can also focus on their specialties which may even be your weaknesses, and so you can follow them at some points in time. But most importantly, you will need to drop your ego right about NOW. Get rid of it. It can not get in your way because leaders have too big of a responsibility. You have a team that is fully relying on your execution and actions.

You also have to know when to keep a close watch and when

you need to loosen up. Again, this goes back to creating micro leaders. There will be times where you will need to have an extreme focus on what your team is doing and how they are going about executing their plans and so on, but there will also come times where you will need to loosen up and trust them to carry out the mission and job properly. Again, a big thing with this is ego. Just let you ego go. It will hold you back forever if you don't let it go. This is one of those things that is hard to find a balance on. But you have to trust your team. And like we talked about before, it would be a whole lot easier to do that if you truly prioritize the process of hiring these team members and business partners.

There always needs to be teamwork. You can not just go out there and complete all the objectives and missions by yourself. It is like in a group project in school. The teams that do the best work are the ones who take the most time to plan out the process on the first day it is assigned. Rather than just winging it, figure out how to distribute the workload. Figure out who is good at what. If Judy is a great designer, than she can be in charge of making the powerpoint presentation. If Bob is a great writer, than he can be in charge of adding the words to the presentation. If Sam is a great entertainer and speaker, than he can give the presentation to the class. Find strengths, then distribute. But don't forget distribute.

Every leader has to deal with finding the proper balance, and it is not an easy task because of the contradictory nature of one extreme and the other. But by understanding that there needs to be a sense of balance, you will be a better leader than most. By practicing the balance and working towards understanding it more and more, you will soon be able to balance the opposing forces of leadership and in turn, you will lead with more influence and efficiency.

Step 9: Mental Toughness

Like we talked about, having the right mindset is HUGE. You will need to be mentally tough in order to be an effective leader and building the right mindset will be absolutely key in order to do that. Leaders are relied on during the toughest times and they are called upon to make important decisions in the heat of the moment. You must be mentally tough in order to make the right choices with a clear conscious and you so that you can put up with the critics.

We already mentioned that leaders are human too, so they will make mistakes. It only makes sense. But what happens when they make those mistakes? Do they blame others, do they take it to offense when others ridicule them and doubt them? No, because leaders don't just own their actions, good or bad. At the same time, they are accepting feedback from team members, other leaders, enemies, haters, and so on. But none of this will take a toll on their mindset nor their confidence. Leaders must be able to hold their confidence, because when you have a company or a team relying on you to lead, you need to be sharp.

Mental toughness also comes into play when we talk about balance. There are going to be some very tough choices that you'll have to make in the heat of every moment. You'll be alone in making the decisions, and the decision can have a direct impact on the rest of the team immediately. So, it is essential that you have a strong and confident mindset to weather these experiences. The nice part is, as you develop over time, you will only get better and better.

Leadership is not for everyone. Some people would rather be lead than to lead. But there are some people who want to lead but they have not yet developed the mental toughness and that is okay. Just stay disciplined and stay hungry, it will develop through you upcoming experiences.

Step 10: Staying Consistent

In reality, this should be a step in every single chapter. But it is just so important for leadership specifically because leaders are not born, they are made. But they also aren't just made overnight. They are made overtime, through a consistent persistent pursuit of becoming the leader you set out to be and envisioned. Again, this step could have been included in every chapter of the book, but the less obvious chapter to have this step is leadership. Because leaders aren't just made and they don't just exist.

There is always a story behind leaders. They developed and shaped themselves into the leader you now see them as. It wasn't magic, it did not happen overnight. But they went through the motions and stayed disciplined for long enough to the point where they began to take ownership and leadership among peer groups and teams. Once that happened, nothing changed. They continued to be consistent. They were relentless. They learned from their experiences, even to this day. No matter where you are at as a leader, you must stay consistent going forward to continue to have an impact and influence on others. Another great quote by John C. Maxwell, an American author, is as follows:

"Small disciplines repeated with consistency every day lead to great *achievements gained slowly over time."* – John C. Maxwell

Well John, you said it damn near perfectly. Becoming a leader is a process. It is a process of growth, discipline, change, and so much more. And there will be many distractions along the process to becoming a leader, but you must stay consistent with how you carry yourself and how you develop into the leader you wish to become.

Consistency is key, but there is also the aspect of account-ability. Are you able to consistently hold yourself accountable for being consistent? Some people can and some people can't, and if you can not, than it isn't a big deal and it also doesn't mean that you can't be a leader. You just need to find someone, like a business partner or a motivated friend, who can help you along the process by holding you accountable. It works best if you are both going through the same process of change and it also works good if the other person has already went through it. Either way, you will need to find some accountability in your life at some point.

Remember what we said in the beginning? Leaders are not born, they are made. But they are also not mad overnight, they are made overtime. It is a damn process! It is a process of growth and change. But you can not grow or change without pressure or without being put in uncomfortable situations. You have to become comfortable with being uncomfortable. Everything you want in life will be a direct result of your willingness to be uncomfortable and that will develop over time. You can only grow and change at a personal level when you are challenged and pushed to go further or to go against the grain. When you are put in tough spots and you break through the pressure and difficulties, that is where growth happens.

Now, are you willing to be patient and consistent in this

process? Are you willing to spend the next 365 days committed to becoming a leader? If you seriously are, than great, good for you. But now you must take action, otherwise everything we talked about would be useless.

Step 11: Adaptability

Remember what we talked about before? The best leaders are not bosses, or people that push other people around. The best leaders care more about the results of the team than anything else. They are people who check their ego at the door, and seek leadership positions for the greater good of the team, not for their own power. Leaders are not only the best leaders, but they are also the best followers. The difference is that they know when to be and when not to be. They are able to adapt to different situations, problems and agendas. They are able to handle high intensity situations and make a decision with their team as the top priority.

Leaders are obviously rare, especially in today's age. And the description and presentation of what it takes to be a leader is all messed up thanks to social media and modern day entrepreneurship. So often, these so called leaders sacrifice their own team and people for their own best interest. Rather than laying people off or firing people or putting the blame on team members, take ownership. Adapt to the situation. You have to adapt to survive, and this is especially true for leadership.

Becoming a better leader requires you to change your identity. Are you able to adjust, change and grow? In college and in high school, we are taught about how things were done up until that day, and in most cases even a few years before that. You know it and I know it, things have changed! A lot has changed! And they will continue to change!

So, what does this mean? Well, you are going to have to adapt to this change. If you aren't able to adapt to these changes, your decisions will then be based on pure emotion. You will panic, and ultimately, you will fail to be the effective leader that your team or organization needs you to be. Adapt now or be left behind, it is that simple.

My Case Study

Step 1 in this chapter was to define leadership. Similar to how most kids and students think, I too had the wrong idea of what exactly a leader was. To most people, especially students or employees early on in their career, they see leaders as people who are very powerful, hard to talk to, and also someone who gives orders to. Well, we got it all wrong. Those people are bosses, not leaders. I knew that to be an entrepreneur and to run a great company, I had to be a leader. But my perception of a leader was that of a boss, and because of that, my first company that I started with 3 of my friends from high school is now down to 1 last person, myself. You can not be a leader if you can't define what it takes to be one! Like all things in this book and in life, it is a learning process, you are not alone.

Step 2 was the process to becoming a leader. Leaders need to set good examples for their team, so the process of becoming a leader is important because it can show your team the work ethic and discipline that goes into developing these skills. Something that helped me a ton with this was reading and studying books from leadership experts, more specifically, Jocko Willink and Simon Sinek. I highly recommend checking out their content.

Step 3 was to take ownership. And this is a principle that was revolutionized by Jocko Willink who we had just mentioned. In his book, the main theme was how leaders need to take ownership. I can honestly say that this core theme from his book *Extreme Ownership* changed my life. Taking ownership is a simple idea in that anyone and everyone can do it without much effort. But it is also essential to becoming a successful leader. You need to own your actions, your decisions, and especially the results, good or bad. For me, once I started to do this, things changed pretty quick. Even for the little things. When my girlfriend broke up with me, I took ownership. And that was not easy to do considering that she was just not a good person. But rather than putting the blame on others, even if they are shitty people, by learning to take ownership if your life, you will soon develop into a better version of yourself. You will begin to see improvements in all areas of your life. It is truly a life changing concept.

Step 4 was influence. The most important quality that a leader has to their team is influence. They have to be able to influence other people to believe in what they are doing, and to get the job done in the most effective way possible. The only way to do this without being a boss as opposed to a leader is through influencing others. Again, this is something that is not taught in schools, so to learn this, you have to make the effort to self educate yourself. Another amazing book that helped to change my life was *How To Win Friends and Influence People* by Dale Carnegie. Isn't it ironic how I am telling you to read other books when I wrote my own book? Well, I know that the books I recommend will better serve your time than textbooks and probably even my book, so definitely check those out. There is no limit to knowledge!

Step 5 was to create your own path. In life and especially in high education, everyone feels the need to be the same and to conform to the artificial boundaries of society that were made up by people that were no smarter than you and I. As soon as I stopped conforming to society, a creative and more ambitious aspect of my brain revealed itself. Try for yourself!

Step 6 was to be of service. This was something that helped me fix something that I was doing repeatedly without even realizing it, which was asking for something rather than asking how you can be of service or give them something. It is all about giving. Once you start to add value to others, you will receive it in ways that are 100x better than before.

Step 7 was to lead and not order. Again, this goes back to the simple definition of what goes into being a good leader. For me, I was always the one to tell people how to do things and tell them what to do, etc. I loved to be in control, and this wasn't necessarily a bad thing. I just wanted to add structure. But I wasn't doing it the right way, I was not implementing influence. So even if things were getting done, the quality wasn't as good because they had no inspiration behind the work.

Step 8 was to have balance. In leadership, decisions are not always easy. There are never extremes, but rather balance. This is possibly the hardest part when developing into a leader. This is also something that you will develop through experience. Just stay consistent and be sure to self reflect and self evaluate.

Step 9 was to have mental toughness. Like I talked about, decisions are going to be tough. You will be caught up in moments that require huge decisions in short time spans. It is especially hard when you have a team relying on you making the right decisions. This is where mental toughness plays a role, and developing this through experience will be key. Get comfortable with being uncomfortable. For me, starting a podcast was the first step in the right decision given that I hated my voice being heard for an hour straight every week publicly.

Step 10 was to stay consistent. This was easy for me after learning the process of goal setting. You should be setting goals for all aspects of your life, including leadership development.

Step 11 was adaptability. The way things have always been done and the way things are starting to be done is wildly different, and it will only continue to change. By exposing yourself to all the right tools and knowledge, you will be prepared to changes.

Chapter 5: The Right Way To Use Social Media

"If people don't know you, they can't flow you." – Grant Cardone

---

Step 1: The Double Edged Sword

Social media is as relevant as ever, with billions of people using one app or another. Social media has really popped off in the last few years, and it is only getting increasingly popular. With this, comes positives and negatives. I like to call social media a double edged sword. It is the perfect example of what a double edged sword means. There is going to be a shit ton of things to talk about in this chapter, and by time you read through it, your outlook, approach and strategies will all be changed.

Let's start with the bad news first. The negative side of the sword. Well, I think we have all noticed that social media has taken a toll on our natural communication skills. For example, walk into Starbucks or any coffee house. What is the first thing you do after ordering your coffee? Yup, you go on your phone and you check social media. Essentially, you are shielding yourself from real world communications and interactions.

Even if you take out your phone and don't use it for social media, it is still a byproduct of social media, due to the inability of real and personal interactions.

Social media is also very addicting. When used, it releases a ton of dopamine, which is an addictive chemical released in the brain. Dopamine is also released when you do things like drugs or even having sex. Again, it is addictive, which is why we turn to social media so often everyday. Now, I don't think this is a terrible thing. There are many people out there that will tell you the horrors of social media and how it is going to destroy society and so on. Relax, everything will be okay, but it is smart to address the issues upfront first.

The other thing that is messed up with social media is the fake influencers. Social media is full of people showcasing fake lifestyles. Because of social media, people are enabled to present themselves in a completely manipulative way. Those accounts you see of kids or young adults showcasing nice cars, private jets, stacks of cash, gold watches, luxury clothing, strippers, mansions, and so on are almost always fraud. They use what I call "community" items, meaning there is one of these cars or shoes or watches and a group of people pass it around for this exact use while none of them actually own it.

It is sad to see, and what is more sad is how these people can make the average person feel so bad about themselves. When the average person on on social media scrolling through their feed and they see these people living their fake ass high end lifestyle, they get all sad and depressed about their own life. This is another huge issue with social media. Because everyone is so vulnerable on it, we decide to compare our lives to those of others. We begin to get depressed, sad, impatient, and in a lot of cases, suicidal because of what is seen on social media.

This is something I struggled with in the beginning, but once you realize that 99% are fake, you will be fine. And also, you will begin to learn that your life is on your own terms and your own timeline. Just because all of this stuff happened for them at 22 years old doesn't mean you are a failure or that you got left behind because it didn't happen for you at that same age. No! You are different. Do not compare your chapter 1 to someone else's chapter 15!

So yeah, there are some negatives of social media, but after reading this chapter, you'll learn how to avoid those and cash in on all of the great byproducts of social media. The most important thing to understand before taking advantage of these great tools is that money follows attention. Yes, read that again. Money follows attention. Well luckily for us, it has never been easier and more accessible to get attention. Social media instantly gives you access to hundreds of millions of people. This is truly remarkable, so we have to learn how to cash in on this.

As Grant Cardone says, if people don't know you, then they can't flow you. How can you make yourself know? Simple, through social media. Social media is amazing because it is free. You can pay for ads, but that isn't always necessary. There are so many ways to grow organically for free, and we will cover each social media platform that I use to grow and how I was able to effectively do it. TV, newspaper, and billboards ads are almost all going extinct. Everything is digital now, right on your smartphone.

Another awesome part about social media is the networking feature. Sure, you might not make the most personal relationships through social media, but just being exposed to the different people and resources out there can go along way. You can easily build your business directly on social media. If you are building a product, you can find your target customers directly on social media and you can even interact with them right then and there.

Because there are both negatives and positives of using social media, you will need to fully understand how to use it, because if you don't understand how to use it, than you will be used by it. You have to choices here, you can either use it to be entertained (be used) or you can learn how to use it to entertain (use it). In this chapter, we will cover everything you need to know about leveraging the right social media platforms to grow your brand the right way.

Step 2: Building Your Brand

So, hopefully by the time you are reading this book or this chapter, building a brand will be as prevalent as it is at the time I am writing this, which is early February 2019. At this time, and for the foreseeable future, building a brand will be absolutely crucial to your overall success and wellbeing in 2019 and years after. You've probably heard this over and over, but what does it truly mean? Well, building a brand is very simple. It is just leveraging social media to portray yourself and what you stand for. It also gives you a platform to share your gifts and passions with the world on an easily accessible medium.

Why is building a brand so crucial? Well sure, everyone IS doing it, so why should you? It is because you not only need to stay relevant, but you also have an incredible opportunity here to create a dream lifestyle in a simple and effective way. Ironically I told you not to follow the crowd in this book, but you should be building a personal brand because even though everyone is doing it, everyone is doing it in their own unique way, so don't call me a hypocrite just yet.

How do I build a brand? Where do I even start? What goes into building my own brand? Yea, everyone has these questions. But it is really a lot simpler than you might imagine. As one of our past podcast guests told us, it takes ZERO effort to be yourself. From the legend himself, Steve Sims, that is.

So, when building a brand, there are really only 3 steps. The first step is to have accounts on all the social platforms, or at least the ones we will discuss later in this chapter. The next step is to just be yourself! And the final step of course is to stay consistent. That is it, that is all it takes to build a brand in 2019! So, don't wait, get started on building your brand today.

Step 3 : How To Become an Influencer

Influencers absolutely took off on social media over the last year or so. Becoming an influencer is as relevant and glamorous as just about anything else you can do on the internet at the moment. It isn't just building your brand, it is much more than that. Influencers are like the modern day versions of celebrities. They have a decently large cult like following in a very specific niche. Becoming an influencer will be a huge advantage for you as you build your brand and your business.

Turns out, just about anyone is capable of becoming an influencer. The most important thing to know is that you will have to start small. Everyone does. And it is going to be all about patience. Yea, it isn't fun when you have 3 YouTube subscribers, 35 Instagram followers and 14 Twitter followers. It sucks in the beginning, and the beginning is always the hardest time. But if you can stay consistent early on, you will see your following grow at a consistent pace over time.

Another very important thing about being an influencer that will last over time and maintain a following is by following the laws of leadership that we discussed. You have to have the ability to influence and inspire. Short term motivation won't cut it anymore. So make sure you are putting out content that inspires others and also shows them that they are just like you, capable of being an influencer and doing amazing things on the internet.

Influencers all start small, but as they grow, they grow fast. Again, the concepts talked about earlier in this book will all apply to these later chapters. Speed matters. You aren't the only one who is trying to build a brand and become an relevant influencer, so speed and momentum won't hurt, but definitely keep your focus on being consistent with putting out great content.

Step 4: The Right Approach

Social media is changing the world forever, and some people are scared. They aren't taking advantage of the amazing benefits, and instead, they are hiding behind their screens. What I see as the most common approach is this: Start a personal page, stay on private, only follow and accept follows from my friends, family, and people that I know and then post 1-2 times per month. This is the typical account of a high school or college student. WHY?!?!?! This is the absolute WORST way to use social media. I used to be that person! I learned the hard way, so I am here to teach you why it is wrong and how to fix it NOW.

First off, why is it wrong? Well, it takes us back to the laws of money. Whether you like it or not, money follows attention. There is no better opportunity for attention than being relevant on social media platforms. We have a unique opportunity to showcase ourselves, our brands, our products and our companies to billions.

This is something so unique and so powerful and people are straight up wasting it like it's nothing! If you want attention in 2019, you are going to need to build your brand on social media. So, turn off the private setting on your account right now. If you are private while reading this, set the book down and change the setting before you continue reading.

In most cases, the people on private are only friends with their closest friends from school and family, as well as a handful of friends and family that they don't see often. That's cute man, but stop. Don't listen to your mom! I guarantee that 90% of your customers will come from social media. You can have your real friends in real life, it is better that way anyways. So, let's start using social media to market ourselves to the other few billion people that aren't our friends.

Step 5: Personal vs. Business Account

So the 3 main platforms we are going to focus on are going to be Instagram, Snapchat, Facebook, and LinkedIn. We will also talk about YouTube and podcasting as a medium, but those 2 don't really apply to this section. So, make sure to have accounts on all 4 of those social media sites. Yes, accounts is plural. That means you will need 2 accounts on each platform, one for your personal brand and one for your business. For some people, their personal brand is their business which is great, but it doesn't hurt to grow 2 accounts simultaneously.

You will also be starting a podcast or a vlog or something of that sort but we will discuss that later on. So on Instagram, you create your own personal page complimented by a company page. On Facebook, you will create your personal profile and then branch off of it by creating an individual page for your business which will be sponsored by your personal page. On Twitter, simply have a personal account and a business account. And on LinkedIn, you will create a personal page, and then sponsor company pages for your own companies.

Now, why does this at all matter? Why do we need multiple accounts on EVERY platform? Well, simple. It is a growth hack. If you can grow 2 accounts at once, they can feed off of each other and grow off of each other. By time someone has an account with 10K followers, you will have 2 accounts with 10K followers, EACH. That is huge! That is months of hard work.

Your company page also needs a personal side to it, so by feeding into your personal page, it helps the users and potential customers on social media to find you and your story. But, like we discussed already, none of these accounts can be on private. Social media is not for talking to your "in real life" friends. Leverage it for business instead, so get off of private!

Step 6: How To Win on Instagram

At the time I am writing this step, Instagram is the hottest platform in the game. Instagram is THE place to be for social media, period. Facebook is still exploding nonetheless but Instagram is the hottest for people like you and me. Now that you understand the importance of social media and the power it holds, we are going to learn how to succeed on each individual platform. A lot of the methods that I will be talking about in the next few pages have been tested and have worked for myself and my close friends and business partners. Some of them are even replicated from the likes of Gary Vee and others that are absolutely crushing the game right now.

Instagram is an awesome platform, and it can be real fun to use. The problem is that most people do not know how to properly grow an organic following, meaning a following for your page that is loyal and authentic. Some people can do this very well when they first start out, but they can not keep growing at a consistent pace, and they fall behind. Their accounts go flatline. I was there too, and most people end up in this spot. It is fine because we can totally rejuvenate this and restart the growth that you all want to see.

First and foremost, make sure that you are a business account. Yes, even if you do not physically own a business. Anyone can have a business account, so go ahead and make your account a business profile if it isn't already. It doesn't cost anything and it takes 3 seconds to change it. With this profile setting, you will gain access to Instagram insights. They aren't the best, but they definitely help. I use them on every one of my posts and stories. But I also use 3rd party resources lie Hype Auditor for a better overall picture of my account. I highly recommend that you look at the insights for each post after a day or so. This will help you to pick up on what specific content is working for you and what isn't. You are also able to see where people are finding your posts, meaning you can pick the best hashtags each time. The insights will help you to deliver the content that your audience is craving. This way, you can steer clear of content that doesn't bring value to your specific niche.

Another simple thing here is picking a niche audience for your page. Who do you want to target, what kind of people? Are you providing motivational content, blogs and vlogs, business to business, and so on. My page is tuned for a podcast audience, specifically college student entrepreneurs. That is a very well defined niche. By picking a small and defined niche, you'll be able to grow faster and become more popular. Pick your page niche and stick with it. There are no limitations here, you can choose any niche you'd like.

Now, let's talk about content. The most important thing that you need to understand is that content is king. Your page's performance and growth relies heavily on the amount and quality of content that you are pumping out. When first starting out, I recommend you post 2 times a day. I started off by posting 1 time per day, but after switching to 2 times per day, it helped boost our page growth in a noticeable way. No excuses, put out at least 1 post a day. There is no reason for not doing so, and if you aren't doing this, then don't expect to grow at all. The best times to post are typically at 9AM, 3PM, and 8PM EST times. But again, use the Instagram insights tools to find out when your specific followers are most active on specific days. Be careful not to post too often though. I would day 3-4 times per day is the most you should be posting. But, be sure to make the most out of Instagram stories and IGTV. I recommend that you post as many stories as possible per day, and at least 1 new IGTV video a week would be ideal.

Now, you understand the importance of consistency and repetition, but you may be wondering what to post, or how to make good content. I can only help you with one of those things, and that is making good content because what you post is all up to you and dependent on your specific niche. When you first start out, I recommend you find one very big and popular page in your niche. For business and entrepreneurship, most people use Gary Vaynerchuk's page for ideas and inspiration. I personally look to Gary, Grant Cardone, and Ed Mylett. There are also a few others I look to as well. But find one or a few pages to look to for inspiration. See what they are posting, how frequently and so on.

Now, you have a good idea for a post but you don't know how to design or make these graphics. Well, same here. If you are a master of design, then good for you. But there is an app for that anyways. You're not surprised, are you? Download the app called Canva. This is an incredibly powerful and useful tool that I use to create graphics for my social media posts. It is not easy to explain without visuals, so I recommend that you get the app or visit the website and sign up for a free account. It is completely free to use. They have templates for posts for all social media platforms, and all you have to do is edit it. For me, I post quotes pictures everyday as well as video snippets from our podcast interviews. I use Canva for the quotes. I simply find a quote I like, I copy and paste it into my template, and I upload an image of whosoever quote it is to the background. It takes me 3 minutes, tops.

So yea, there is absolutely no excuse for not posting at least once a day. And again, you'll need to test and test again to find what works best for you. I tested tons of different templates and styles before deciding to stick with the one I use now. Engage with your audience, constantly look at the insights, and make decisions on the fly. The videos are a little more difficult to make, as there is a learning curve to them. I use an app called InShot, which is not free, but totally worth it. It takes some time to learn, but like everything in this book, you'll need to put some real time and effort into everything you do if you wish to become successful.

Now, you got your profile set up the way it should be, you are posting great content frequently, so what else is there? Well, a whole lot more! Another very important thing with Instagram is to respond to every single comment that you get on your posts. It may be easy now with 2-3 comments on your posts, but keep doing this even when you get to 50-100 comments per post like I get. It is easy to do and it pays off big time. Also stay on top of your DMs, just another very simple yet effective tip.

Another thing that I do everyday before I go to bed is I go to the explore page. This is where the top posts relating to your activity and your page will show up. The goal for your posts is to show up on the explore page. Only one of my posts has ever showed up there, so don't expect anything to happen for you right away. But, if you do show up there, it pays off big time, as I gained 1K followers that day. While on the explore page, go through each posts, commenting and liking each one. Write a meaningful comment. By consistently doing this, you are engaging with top posts that people will see, and your comments may rise to the top of the post if they are well received and liked by enough viewers of that post.

Another great growth hack for Instagram is joining engagement groups. These are groups in your DMs where a handful of similar accounts from your niche will send their most recent posts. Once they send their post, everyone in the group, usually 10-20 accounts, will go to that post to give it a like and a comment. The Instagram algorithm favors engagement heavily, and receiving it consistently from similar accounts goes a long way. These groups can help dramatically increase engagement and growth for your account. They typically cost a few dollars, but I plan on creating a few groups for the readers of this book, so be sure to send me a DM on Instagram if you are interested in joining the engagement group for free of course.

It is also a good idea to find a few more to join, because the more engagement the better.

Another great way to grow is through shoutouts. There are 2 types of shoutouts. Paid shoutouts and then S4S, which are shoutouts for shoutouts. These are typically put on your story. Paid shoutouts are great and they can help you to grow quick, but they can also add up and become super expensive. I still believe that they are more valuable than running Instagram ads, so it is not a bad idea to check them out. Be careful, though. You will want to get shoutouts from large accounts in your niche, but check their accounts. Make sure their engagement is high. Also, ask them to send you the follower demographics information. You want to avoid getting shoutouts from accounts with a majority Indian following because they are the cheapest followers. S4S are great for smaller accounts as well, since they are free and can be done an unlimited amount. Simply find a few accounts that are decent or the same size as your account and ask them if they are interested in doing a S4S. Be sure to message a handful of accounts because not only will some not answer, but it also does not hurt to do multiple if that is a possibility. Always work for more exposure!

Starting out is a slow process, and patience will play a major role. Countless hours will go into this at the beginning, but understand that it will all pay off, it just might take 6-12 months. Don't quit! You must keep going. I promise you that if you post 1 time per day and follow the rest of my tips and tricks that I shared, your life and business will dramatically get better in a year. Remember the core principle of this chapter, money follows attention!

Step 7: How To Win on Twitter

Twitter is another great platform, and it's one that you probably use for personal and casual purposes. Again, let's flip that around. The whole mindset here is to capitalize on the monetary possibilities with these platforms. It doesn't mean you can't have fun on social media. You can still keep a personal account and follow all your friends and so on. I do that too. But it is a great idea to make a new page for your business or product or whatever it is you want to help promote more.

Twitter is definitely not as hot as Instagram is right now. Twitter is probably the least booming in the game right now, but we all know it'll come back around soon, so we might as well get a head start. The nice thing with all of these platforms is that you can focus on one to start, I'd recommend it being Instagram, and then you can branch out over time. It is good to have set up accounts on all platforms just so that they are there, but I definitely recommend that you go all in on one of these platforms for a few months. If you go hard on Instagram and you get 5K followers after 3 months, it'll make it that much easier to grow your Twitter. You can noe point 5K people to your Twitter account instantly. This is a great growth hack across all platforms. So, don't feel as if you have to go all in on each platform I mention here, but definitely keep in mind how you will attack them all later on.

So, Twitter is different than Instagram in that it is centered around words and phrases. There is an exponentially higher amount of posts, or as Twitter calls them, tweets. Because of this, it will be that much harder to stand out and get noticed. Unlike Instagram, there is no explore page. So this will be a grind from the start. Expect to grow slowly for the first few months, but like with all things, once you have a solid base, you will be ready for some killer growth.

Again, content is king and this is the consistent truth across all of the platforms that I will mention. For Twitter though, quantity is much more important than quality. First of all, making high quality tweets doesn't take much effort like with Instagram. For Instagram, you need a fire post with a good caption and proper use of hashtags etc. But for Twitter, it is simply a 280 character limit text box. You can also add images and links and I will get into that. Since Twitter is so large and there is such a high quantity of tweets being sent out every second, quantity will be key. To stand out and to get noticed, you have to put yourself out there the most, or as frequent as possible. I think that the sweet spot with tweets is 5-10 good tweets as well as 5-10 responses per day. Responding to influencers and bigger accounts in your niche help a ton as well, as long as you are making sure that they are thoughtful and meaningful responses that can add value to others. This is still pretty low, so you can double that if you wish, but as I said, it will be hard to focus on growing multiple social media streams, so it may be best to start small and focus on Instagram. Nevertheless, there is no excuse as to why you can not send out 3 tweets a day.

Another great thing about Twitter is that you can stand out pretty easily, you just have to think for yourself. Tweets are essentially thoughts written out as tweets, so if you are being open and honest about yourself and putting out the content that you want to put out, you'll have no problem gaining a unique following on Twitter. Engagement groups work, shoutouts work, and engaging with others work, but it all about quantity with Twitter. Be seen! Remember, this is a long term battle, so don't give up early on. Happy tweeting!

Step 8: How To Win on Facebook

To be honest, I am not very knowledgeable with Facebook, only because it was never a big focus for me. Facebook is definitely losing steam to Instagram, and I also see Twitter or even LinkedIn cutting deeper into their user base and engagement volume that they have going on right now. It just was never worth it to me to go all in on Facebook. But, Facebook owns Instagram, so there are some connections there and some things that you can do to enhance your experience on both of the platforms.

Since Facebook owns Instagram, you are able to link your Instagram business profile to a Facebook business page. So, if you do not have Facebook or you do not have a Facebook business page, be sure to sign up for one. This will allow you to runs ads on Instagram, which can be extremely helpful. Running ads on Instagram allows you to reach a broad audience over a short amount of time, and as of right now, the rates are cheap for the amount of impressions and views your page or promotion will receive from the ad.

Enough on Instagram, though. Facebook can be great for you, especially if you are a younger kid like I am who has parents actively on Facebook, because you can basically get free shoutouts, known as post shares on Facebook, from your parents and family members. Be professional and show your older relatives that you are working on something meaningful and that you deserve their full support. By them sharing your first few posts, you can pick up a good amount of new friends. Boom, you just jump started your growth on Facebook. And before this book, you probably never even had a Facebook to begin with.

Now that you have a prominent personal page with decent exposure and a decent sized friend network, you can create your first business page for whatever it is that you are working on or selling. This is easy to do, and you can use the same information from your Instagram or even from your website. You can add buttons to the front page of the profile for people to be directed to your website or your app or your products and so on. You can then start to invite your friends to like and follow the page. Boom, you are well on your way now!

After you have a solid base for both your business and personal Facebook pages, let's shift focus to the 2 best features that Facebook has. The first that I will talk about is live video. Live video is popping off on all platforms, but as of right now, nothing compares to Facebook live video in terms of quality and in terms of exposure. Instagram is right behind them, but right now, make sure to master live videos on Facebook. Live videos might be scary for you at first, but who cares. Like with all things in this book, just get it done! That will be the only way for you to level up. You need to take full advantage of all the tools and tricks that I discuss in this book. I don't want to lecture you, I want to equip you.

The next tool on Facebook that can be super helpful for business pages and for personal brands is the Facebook groups feature. These are popping off as well, so make sure to get in on the action. There are thousands of Facebook groups out there, but it might also be a good idea to create your own group as well. If you are slowly able to grow this overtime while staying consistent in the group with new content and updates, you will soon have a nice following there that you can tap in to directly at any given moment.

So, even though Facebook is resorted for mostly the older generation, it is still extremely important to have a presence there. Focus on Instagram, but check up on Facebook often.

Step 9: How To Win on YouTube

Like with Facebook, I was never an expert at YouTube. Until recently with my podcast Real Talk University, I never had a YouTube channel and I was always just a user rather than a provider. When I realized that you can't win as a user, I immediately took action and began my journey as a provider. I just recently started our podcast YouTube page, and with that, I have been putting up all of our audio interviews on our YouTube pages as video interviews as well. I originally only recorded audio, but I quickly made the switch to doing video interviews after realizing that I was missing out on a large audience. I will talk more about podcasting as a medium in the next step of this chapter.

YouTube is pretty straightforward. I would say that there are 3 key aspects to being successful early on. The first is to have an appealing thumbnail, which is the cover art that you see for the videos when you search them or see them on the home page. I use Canva for this, which I previously mentioned, and it is super easy to create thumbnails that pop. The next thing is to use good tags and keywords for your videos so that they are relevant. I suggest using Uber Suggest to search what is trending. It is a tool created by Neil Patel. The last thing is to have quality video content on a consistent basis. At first, I would recommend just putting out regular videos. When you get further into the process, you can then outsource the video editing to professionals so that your video quality is top notch.

I regret not starting on YouTube years ago, as one of our past interviews on the podcast had told us that it was super easy to get thousands of views and thousands of subscribers on YouTube just a few years ago. But it is still early, and YouTube still has room to grow, so make sure that you get on it as soon as possible.

Step 10: How To Win at Podcasting

So, podcasting isn't really a form of social media, it is more of a media outlet, but since it has become so relevant and since it has had such an impact and lasting change on my life, I figured we could take about how you can start your very own podcast today as well. Because podcasting is becoming so mainstream, there has never been a better time to get started, and I truly believe that every college student should launch their own podcast. By starting your own podcast, you are creating the opportunity for yourself to be extremely credible and relevant in whatever area of work or passion you are into. Podcasting also gives you a platform to share your voice and your message. So, what is your excuse?

When I started my podcast, Real Talk University, with my best friend from college, neither of us had a clue of how the process worked. We just winged it. We decided that rather than waiting and procrastinating for days thinking of the best way to start, we could just start that same day and get the shitty first episode recorded. Even the best podcasters like Tim Ferriss for example, will always remind their listeners of how horrendous their first episode was looking back on it. All that matters right now it to push out content. Focus on that and the quality will start to come once you develop your own unique approach.

Best decision yet. By taking immediate action on an idea or a plan, great things will happen, and since I made that decision, great things have indeed happened. Look at this beautiful book for example!

Now, how do you start a podcast exactly? Well, most people assume that you need some sort of high level podcasting equipment. You don't! All you need right now is your phone, seriously. If you have an iPhone, than you can put out your podcast in the next 5 minutes if you really wanted to. All you need is the app called Anchor.fm. Now, sadly they do not have any affiliate codes or incentives for me because it is insane how many times I recommend this app to people. I should just work for them already. They also just got bought out by Spotify at the time I am writing this, so that will be huge for them and all their users.

If you are too lazy to find out what Anchoor.fm does, then I will sum it up for you real quick. It is basically a free app that allows you to record audio directly from your cell phone and turn it into a podcast. You can create your podcast directly on the app, including the podcast name, tagline, cover art, and more. It is legit. And once you publish your first episode, it will automatically put your podcast on directories such as Apple Podcasts, Spotify, Stitcher, and on their own podcast streaming service as well of course. Again, this is all completely free and requires nothing but a smartphone and a partial brain.

There are a few key decisions to make when starting a podcast, but perhaps the most crucial will be to define your niche. This is where you'll decide WHO your podcast is for. There are millions of podcasts out there so you will need to stand out in some way or another, and focusing on a small niche audience is the absolute best way to do that. Take some time and really think about what it is that interests you, and what audience you want to serve. It is also best to focus on a smaller niche, rather than something like "Entrepreneurship", try something more like "Middle Eastern Entrepreneurship", a more well defined niche.

So, I definitely recommend you get started on your podcast journey as soon as you can. It is so simple to do and there is really no excuse for you not to get in on the action. Remember, money follows attention. It is one of the concrete laws of money and wealth. So, if you wish to be wealthy one day, than it is in your best interest to utilize all of the tools I have talked about thus far.

So again, there is no reason not to at least give podcasting a fair try. You might not nail it down right away, and neither did we. But you'll never grow or change in life if you are not putting yourself in uncomfortable situations. Seek discomfort! Progress is everything. If you wait for things to align perfectly, than you will wait your entire life. We all have flaws, but those flaws are what make us unique, relatable and allows us to continually create new content without having fear of perfection.

The neat thing with all of this is that everything I have talked about can build off of each other. You can start wherever you wish, although I do recommend making Instagram a priority. By building an audience on one platform, you can begin to leverage that audience to branch out into other mediums such as podcasting, or YouTube videos and so on. They will all begin to build on each other. In the beginning it will take a lot of time because you will be starting from zero, nothing at all. But once you start to build an audience on a few platforms, you will skyrocket in growth, and I can not wait for it to happen for all of you!

You may think that social media is still just that tool you use to check up on your friends and to waste time while your bored or before bedtime, but I promise you, that if you take the tips and discussions from this chapter seriously, then it can alter your life forever. It is pretty stupid how easy it is to cash in on social media, but since the opportunity is there and you are already spending a ton of time on it nowadays, why not take advantage of that time and make some money from it? That is the question you should be considering. Why not? There is no answer to that, so get started. Build that social media empire from the ground up today!

Step 11: How To Win on LinkedIn

LinkedIn is a very interesting platform, and it wasn't until recently that I was able to capitalize on the amazing organic reach. Not only is the reach incredible, but the quality of the audience on LinkedIn is better than any other platform out there. The organic reach of LinkedIn right now, in 2019, is comparable to that of Facebook before ad manager was rolled out.

LinkedIn is starting to become a content-centric platform, which provides a unique opportunity for people like you and me to become a true influencer on this platform. Try this, picture a recruiter or executive at a high-level company. Imagine that they are preparing to interview YOU for a high-level position. There is a 99.9% chance that they'll check out your LinkedIn profile prior to the interview. Imagine how that interview will go now that they have seen that you are an absolute stud on LinkedIn. I guarantee that if you follow this strategy then this mock situation will be a common story among WTWTY readers.

Okay, now let's dive into the basics of setting your profile up for success. The profile picture is a good place to start. Be sure to use a clear and professional looking picture or portrait of yourself. Make sure it is a high-quality picture of you, with nobody else in it. The next step is your profile headline. This is as simple as stating what you do and who you do it for. For the media on your profile, be sure to upload resumes, articles, publications, or anything else that you'd like to be highlighted.

As for posting on LinkedIn, there are 2 rules that you must follow to find success. The first rule is to post consistently. Like with any other platform, you have to be posting frequently so that you are not forgotten about. The second rule is to provide value in all of your posts. Rather than bloating or talking about yourself, figure out a way to add value to others. If you had an experience at work, share it! But what were the lessons learned? How can others benefit from reading this story or happening?

Another way to get more engagement on your posts is to add around 6-12 hashtags at the bottom of your post. Keep these related to the copy of your post or the niche you'd like to target in general. You'll also want to be sure to reply to ALL comments that are left on your post. Show your audience that you actually CARE.

If you want engagement on your posts then you have to engage with other posts first. Give before you receive. Engaging with posts throughout the day will catapult the growth of your page. It is a really simple concept but it'll be key to your growth.

So, how do you go about doing this? Simple. Check up on LinkedIn every few hours. While you're there, read some posts that appear on your feed. If you see something interesting and you have something to say then simply leave a comment with your thoughts on that post. The best way to go about doing this is to add to the post. If they made a post about the best practices to growing on LinkedIn, then share some of your own best practices that might not have been mentioned. One rule: Never leave a negative comment. Positivity and optimism ONLY.

My Case Study

Step 1 in this chapter was to be aware of the double edged sword that is social media. There are definitely 2 sides to social media, and I think that most people know one side better than the other, which is how social media is dangerous, addicting, and so on. But I truly do not think it has to be that way, and the other side of the sword is so valuable to pass up on. For me, social media would always be the wrong side of the sword growing up. The worst aspect is when I used to compare myself to others through social media. Almost everyone in middle school and high school years goes through this, but it wasn't until my first year in college where I picked up on this and I decided to flip the switch. Best decision ever, and I wish I made it earlier in life.

Step 2 was the importance of building a brand in 2019 and beyond. It has become so important to promote yourself and promote some sort of story or selling point about yourself, and with social media, the barrier to entry to do this is non existent. I was worried at first that I couldn't build a brand because I didn't really have a story yet. I mean, not too many people have out all figured out at 19 years old. But that didn't matter, because it opened up another way to build a brand and a following and that was to document the process. As long as you are real, honest, and transparent with your following, you can grow a brand successfully in anyway you wish.

Step 3 was how to become an influencer. So, this is like how do you become a successful product or a successful company. It will take time! But the same rules about building a brand relate to becoming an influencer, and that is being real, transparent and honest with your audience. The best part is that it takes absolutely no effort to be yourself! For me, this was a slight struggle at first, especially when we had some failures early on. But I found it best to be on open book, and to share those failures as well. Who knows, there could be some others going through that same thing and by sharing your failures and admitting your mistakes, you can influence them to do the same or to learn from you. Influence!

Step 4 was to find the right approach. This one was simple for me and it can be simple for you. Expose yourself. Get off of a private account, now!

Step 5 was deciding between having a personal account versus a business account. Easy, I will make that decision happen for you. Both! You will definitely want to have both. You can build your brand through a company page, a brand page, movement page, etc but definitely stay active on a strictly personal account and make sure to make your audience aware of that personal account so they know who is behind the brand. I have this set up and always have had it.

Step 6 was winning on Instagram. I used to use Instagram to post once in a blue moon. I would simply use it to be entertained, but I flipped the switch and because of that, my life changed. It is such a powerful tool for any business or personal brand, and it is most definitely worth the investment of $0. LOL!

Step 7 was winning on Twitter. Same thing with Twitter and with all social media platforms. In my case, I was always on social media to be entertained. Well, remember our money law? MONEY FOLLOWS ATTENTION! Twitter has been a super helpful tool to me, especially because I can easily grow multiple accounts at the same time and then use each of the accounts to help grow the others.

Step 8 was winning on Facebook. Oh yea, the grandma platform? I thought the same thing as well. Why in the world would I join Facebook, my parents are on there! Funny enough, you can use that to your advantage immediately. When I made a Facebook, I used my parents account to share my posts, and I grew an audience a lot faster than most people do.

Step 9 was YouTube. I never truly understood YouTube. Mostly all of these social media platforms were foreign to me up until late in 2018. But YouTube was like that up until early 2019, unfortunately. Do not wait to get started on these platforms, you WILL regret it! Every day you wait, it will get that much harder to win.

Step 10 was podcasting. Me doing a podcast was something I could have never envisioned, given that I sucked at speaking, was afraid to share my thoughts with friends, and so on. So, I'd like to say I am a changed man because of this experience thus far. It has helped me to create lasting connections with absolute legends that I used to idolize, and it has helped me to improve myself in so many ways. It was a big risk and a big leap of faith for me, but it worked and I couldn't be more grateful or more blessed to be where I am today because of it.

Step 11 was regarding LinkedIn. I have to get out in front of this and say that this step was not in the original manuscript. I never cared for LinkedIn, mostly because I didn't understand how to use it the right way. But over these past 3 months, it has been my #1 platform in terms of lead gen, building meaningful connections, and building a loyal audience. Who would have thought?!?! This just emphasizes my point that you have to keep all options open. Things in this space are always changing, and attention is always moving to new platforms. You must be able to adapt. Follow my formula and you'll be a top performer on LinkedIn in no time!

Chapter 6: Why NOW Is The Best Time To Invest In Yourself

"Be patient with yourself. Self-growth is tender; it's holy ground. There's no greater investment." - Stephen Covey

---

Step 1: The Power of NOW

This is an awesome chapter topic that I have been so excited to write about since I started this book journey a little over a month ago. This is just so crucial, and it is one of my biggest passions. It gets me going, it excites me! So, given the chapter title, you understand where this chapter is going. In 2019, the time that we are living and growing up in, is going to be looked back at as the BEST time ever to invest in yourself. Technology is changing fast, social media has played a role bigger than anyone can imagine, and believe it or not, opportunity is overflowing. It is out there. You need to prep, and you need to ready yourself, and the best way to do that is through personal development and investing in yourself.

But you have to start NOW! Not tomorrow, not next week. NOW! There is no excuse to not get started now, as it is so easy, so cheap (as in it is free most of the time.) But, also so crucial and important to you reaching success and your ultimate destination. Understand this: Every single day, every single minute, every single hour that you wait and put things off, the journey and the end goal will become that much harder to reach. Make it easy for yourself, get started now rather than later. By taking massive action now, you will build confidence and momentum to get you going in the direction that you need to be headed, and congratulations, because by reading this book, you are already well on your way. By reading this book, I can assure you that you have the mindset, you have the drive, and you have the ambition to get to where you want to be.

You want to achieve greatness, and we will achieve it together if you listen closely. Out of the 1 million copies of this book that will be sold, only 100,000 will read it. Of that 100,000, only 10,000 will act on the information and tools that I provide. So, it is your choice. Do you want to be among the 1% that buys the book, reads the book, and then actually applies the book to his or her life or do you want to be part of the 99% that busy the book, maybe reads it, and then never applies it? I *know* you want to be part of that 1%. If you made it this far in the book, I know for sure that you want to be a part of that 1% and that you will do what it takes.

It is similar to what Gary Vee says as well. People ask him all the time about why he puts out all of his content when other people in his industry make livings off of selling courses and coaching similar to that which he provides in his videos. Gary answered the question by saying that it didn't matter to him that he was sharing his secret because he knew that even if tens of millions of people watch/read/listen to it, only 1% or less would actually apply it to their own lives and their own businesses and he is 100% correct on that.

There is never going to be that perfect window of time for you to start. Things won't just fall in the right place for you to do what you want to do. Your product will never be perfect. Your song will never be perfect. Your podcast will never be perfect. Your app will never be perfect. Your website will never be perfect. But, more importantly, none of things will matter at all if you don't at least share them and put them out. Start NOW. Start TODAY. Go out there and do what you need to do to get what you want, because you know exactly what you need to do. Let's go!

Step 2: Why Your Need To Be Proactive

NOW is the time to invest in yourself and NOW is the time to be proactive about it. Look, I am in college and I understand why most people are there and why most people go. But, what I don't understand is that these students are willing to study for hours and days on stuff like chemistry, astronomy, calculus, and all that other bullshit curriculum more willingly than they are willing to learn about money. Sure, you're most likely paying a pretty penny to attend college and take those courses, but what happens when you leave?

Well, a majority of students who attend college will take on debt. Funny enough, that is where they leave you off at. They will send you into the real world with a backpack of debt, and no tools or education on how to even get rid of it. There really is no system in place to teach this stuff, and you do NEED to know it because that debt is NEVER leaving you. You are trapped in now, because you can't even declare bankruptcy against student debt now. It will literally go with you all the way to your grave.

Now, I don't mean to scare you or worry you, but I do want to make you more aware of what is actually happening now because most people don't truly get it even if they say they do. Now, you have piled up $200K in debt after getting your masters in business marketing. Wow, congratulations on your great success! Now, you take that piece of paper and you use it to get a good job, one that will pay $60K a year. Well, if you take that job then you will be broke. See, you still have $200K to pay off and you're only making $60K a year. There is also interest on that $200K and I promise you that it will add up faster than you could ever imagine. Then, ten years go by, you have a wife/husband and kids and you finally pay it off. Ten years after getting your piece of paper, you can finally KEEP that $60K that you make because of your degree.

This case is way too common. It is sickening and just sad to witness happen over and over again without people taking notice or making any effective changes. This is why you absolutely must be proactive about investing in yourself. Nobody is going to hold your hand in life and help you out of these types of situations. College might hold your hand and walk you through their curriculum, but where do they go after that? You have to remember that college is a business. They are in the business of making money.

So, it is in your best interest to learn about these things before you have to face them in life. Get a head start. I can't imagine how shitty of a feeling it is after you finish six years of harsh and intense schooling and then you have to work and be extremely loyal for another ten years to finally start making some money. That just sounds so terrible, but it is happening to a majority of graduates because a lot of people are clueless and uneducated.

There are so many ways to be proactive about these kinds of

things as well. You have time now. If you are still in college, you absolutely have time. Make it your goal to graduate debt free, you literally can do this with the help of the internet and all the amazing opportunities it has opened us up to. Start a side hustle and make a few racks a year, it will help. More importantly, educate yourself about the financials, how to pay off debt, how to build your line of credit to a good standing point, and so on.

All of these things matter just as much as that biology test that you have tomorrow or the statistics project that is due this week. It matters, but it doesn't get the attention it deserves, so it is all in your hands to be proactive and alert about things like these.

Step 3: How To Invest In Yourself

So, you finally made the right choice and you want to start to invest in yourself, but how do you do it? There are so many different ways to go about it, some good and some bad. It can be quite overwhelming with the overflow of resources and education that is available to us outside of the classroom. You can invest in yourself for no money at all and you can invest in yourself with a few hundred dollars and either way will work perfectly fine. We will get into the best ways of doing so next.

The way I started was with books. Books can cost anywhere from $3 to $20. You can buy a used book for dirt cheap or you can buy a brand new hardcover book for $20 or $30. Either way, it is worth it, no doubt. People are willing to drop hundreds of dollars on school textbooks that they barely touch during the semester but they aren't willing to spend a few bucks on a book that will teach them more than their entire MBA curriculum will teach.

The first business book I ever read was *Steve Jobs* by Walter Isaacson. This is kind of ironic that you are reading my book and I am telling you to read other books, isn't it? Well not really because you'll want to read numerous books to get the education and skill sets to succeed.

The next business book I read and recommend was *The 22 Immutable Laws of Marketing* by Al Ries and Jack Trout. My grandfather gave me this book and it was an absolute game changer. This is the first time in my life that I started to think with a business and entrepreneurial mindset.

The next business book that I read and recommend was *How To Win Friends and Influence People* by Dale Carnegie. I was a freshman in high school, and I remember hiding the cover when I was reading it in class or in school because I was embarrassed and didn't want people to think that I didn't have any friends. But I have to say, this book is a must read for any high school or college student. Read this book as early in your life as possible. You'll revisit it numerous times as well.

I then began to read numerous more books but the other books I wanted to point out were *Start With Why* by Simon Sinek, *Think and Grow Rich* by Napoleon Hill, and *Rich Dad Poor Dad* by Robert Kiyosaki. If you want to go even further into it, there are newer books that are great such as *Sell or Be Sold* by Grant Cardone, *Crushing It!* by Gary Vaynerchuk, *The 10X Rule* by Grant Cardone, *Extreme Ownership* by Jocko Willink, and so much more. There are way too many books to be named here, but you'll have to read these first and then find some similar ones to your interest. These books can all be bought on Amazon for less than $2 used. You can also find a friend that wants to read and you guys can swap books to save you 50%. But, it is absolutely critical that you get into the habit of reading.

Now let's talk about free education outside of the classroom. The first and most obvious would have to be YouTube. There is literally an endless amount of education on YouTube, but you have to be selective about how you sue it like we previously discussed. YouTube can be entertaining and that is what most will use it for, but there is so much more available to you by using YouTube, it is scary! There are new video uploads everyday by a majority of the authors that I had just mentioned. There are even great book reviews for some of those books, and some have chapter by chapter walkthroughs which can be a great refresher to revisit an old book that you read a while back. It is literally endless education. YouTube is pure gold, and it can even serve to be your first mentor. We haven't yet talked about mentors much, but we will cover it in more detail soon. But, YouTube can definitely serve as your first mentor. Let's be honest, in a few years, virtual mentors will be the way to go.

At this point, you have a TON of resources and homework to do. You really don't need more, but I am going to give it to you anyways. First is podcasts. I know we talked about being on the opposite end and being the one who dishes out podcasts., but you can also listen to others and learn a ton. My podcast, Real Talk University, has been able to help a ton of people since we started, like I hope this book will do. But, I always listen to other people's podcasts as well. I learn how to make mine better and I also learn great things through professionals and life coaches such as Ed Mylett, Lewis Howes, Andy Frisella, to name a few. Podcasts can be a great way to go for people who are always driving or need something to listen to at work. I prefer them over audiobooks because they are more entertaining without loss of quality or education, making them easier to consume while multitasking.

The last avenue we will discuss are courses. Courses are tough because there are so many of them, so you will need to do your own research on what will work best for you. There are a ton of scams and shit courses out there so please be sure to do careful research and talk to current users or clients about their experience. Some of the courses I used to buy were Cardone University (which was about $60 a month), Tai Lopez social media courses (about $50 one time fee). These types of courses can be life changing and can be the best value for your dollar, while others can be a total waste. The only one I can truly recommend is Cardone University. Make sure that you spend your next $60 on that.

Well, now you have millions of hours and pages and audios and videos to dive into. Test some of them out and see what works best for you and then GO ALL IN. Best of luck!

Step 4: Work For FREE

As I am writing this, one of the hottest and highest trending entrepreneurs in the entire game right now just said in an interview that if he had the opportunity, he would work for free for Jeff Bezos, who is the founder and CEO of Amazon, just so that he can see how Jeff is wired and how he does things over at Amazon.

The man who said that was Gary Vaynerchuk. Vaynerchuk is one of the most well known and successful digital entrepreneurs of our time, and he said with certainty that he would drop everything that he is doing right now to work for free for Jeff Bezos for one year.

This really opened up my eyes to the power and importance of surrounding yourself with people who do and have the things you want. There is really no better way to do it, proximity to power is so crucial, but you will need to be willing to make sacrifices, such as working for free. Just remember, every penny, every minute, and every ounce of effort that you are investing in yourself or towards your future will pay itself back 100x.

First of all, if you are just starting out like I am, you don't need to go around asking the Jeff Bezos's of the world to work for them for free, because in reality, that's far stretched. Please, go ahead and reach out to them still because you really do never know. It is always worth reaching out. It costs nothing and the potential ROI is monstrous. But if you are just getting into the game, then there are endless amounts of people to surround yourself and get around that can have an extreme benefit for you and your goals.

Again, I never really realized the magnitude of potential and opportunity that is out there, but having a presence in the digital world in areas such as Instagram, Snapchat, Facebook, Twitter and so on. I have come across so many world class entrepreneurs that I never heard of and they are all doing absolutely incredible things.

There are also your local entrepreneurs and business owners. These guys are typically your best place to start, given that they are in your area. One thing to note, if you are a student in high school or college, you NEED to take advantage of that status and leverage it! Just by being a local student, your chances of finding an opportunity like this increase ten fold. For everyone else, don't lose hope, it's just part of the everyday grind, nothing new.

The best way to approach these people is to figure out what they need help with. Study their business, study their track record and their staff and how their company operates. Then, identify the hole and be the solution to fill it. For example, for a majority of local restaurant chains, they have a great business with great food and so on, but most are lacking a social media presence. If this is a business you'd like to get into, then offer to give them a hand with their social media for FREE. Chances are, they'll pay you after the first month.

Here is another prime example. If there is a page or an influencer on social media that you follow and like, find out how YOU can help THEM get better. It can be in terms of productivity, saving time, saving money, and so on. The key is to get CREATIVE. Isn't that kind of the entire theme of the book? Message 100 of your favorite Instagram influencers and offer to make them content for their page. Send them some of your work. One or two of them will love what you do and bring you on board.

That is all it takes! Find out how YOU can bring value to THEM. For FREE. Follow that formula and you will literally be catapulted in the direction you are trying to go in your career. Getting that type of experience under your belt is invaluable. Go out there and GET IT!

Step 5: Comparing The ROIs

First of all, for those who don't know what ROI is, it stands for Return On Investment. It is the measure of what you get out after putting in something, such as work or money in general. This is the mindset you should always be thinking with. Always ask yourself before making a decision, what is the potential ROI by making this decision? Is there even an ROI by doing this? Sure, not everything can have an ROI. Most of the things you do now probably don't have an ROI, it is probably a 50/50 split. Our goal is to get that to 90/10 split.

By thinking in terms of ROI, you will rewire your brain to make smarter decisions in real time. There are always those times of conflict that we deal with, where we can't make a decision on what to do or when to do it and so on. Simple fix, think in terms of ROI!

Obviously this can be applied to every area of your life, but I want to narrow it down to focus in on time management. There is so much to do and so much to get done each and everyday, and I know that it can be tough to prioritize things and make all of the right decisions. It is something that I struggle with everyday along with everyone else on the planet. Think about college and then think about the things we have talked about in this book so far. If you put ALL of your time and effort to get a degree and good grades, then what is the ROI on that? The ROI chart for this case is basically a plateau. It's flat lined, there isn't anything really extraordinary that can happen as a result of your perfect grades and degree. Maybe in some cases, but not in most. Now again, that isn't saying that you shouldn't get good grades and focus in school or finish your degree and so on. But, you shouldn't put all of your eggs into that basket. You have to split it up. Put some into a side hustle. Put some into personal development. These are both two categories that can have hockey stick looking graphs for their ROI. The potential is through the roof if you can dedicate just a few minutes or hours a day to these two tasks. The ROI of reading Rich Dad Poor Dad is again, like a hockey stick. By reading that book, you are spending maybe $10 as well as around five to ten hours of your time. After that, your life may be changed for good. That book has impacted and changed thousands of people's lives.

Another example is Cardone University, another personal development course that we talked about. It might cost you around $75 and 100+ hours of your time and focus, but the ROI is insane! I was just recently at the 10X Growth Conference in Miami, FL and there was a segment in which ordinary people like you and I went up on the stage and talked about the ROI that they got from investing into Cardone University. The stories absolutely blew me away. Clearly, lives were changed and businesses were completely flipped around, or as Grant likes to say, 10X'ed.

So, when you are making daily decisions, think about what it will return for you. This also goes back to investing in yourself through things like advertisements and promotions via social media. At first, I had a hard time spending $20 on an Instagram shoutout. But when I thought of that investment in terms of the potential ROI, I realized that the $20 I just spent could seriously come back ten fold if I had the patience and continued to build my brand like I was doing. It always will come back to your mindset, and that is why we started the book with that because it is so crucial for people to have in check and optimized.

Now that you are thinking in terms of ROI, keep a journal of the big decisions you make. Tell yourself why you made that decision and then what you expect to get out of it. But also, don't do things just because you expect to get a benefit from doing it. Some things have zero ROI but need to get done regardless. Anyways, continue to hold yourself accountable. 10X!

Step 6: Knowledge is Power

This is a very common saying and it is more true right now than it ever was before. More importantly, this is amazing news for you and me. Because knowledge is so easy to access in today's age at a very large scale, there is a super low barrier level to access power. Literally any of us can equip ourselves with the tools and the knowledge to have power. What kind of power? The most important kind of power, in my opinion, would be influence over others. If you simply have the power to lead a group of people or influence them or convince them to buy certain products from you and so on, you are powerful.

Knowledge can get you very far, but it takes effort because of the way the education system is currently set up. College and high school education means no harm, but they truthfully are years behind modern technology and where education should be at and it is sad to see so many people spending five or six figures a year on higher education and then freeze or hesitate away from buying a webinar or a course online from someone who is earning seven or eight figures a year from the internet. Knowledge is power! Would you rather learn from a professor, who has all of the knowledge you need to be exactly that, a professor, or would you rather learn from some 20 year old kid on Instagram who has grown 10+ accounts to 100K followers and makes over seven figures a year passively? For me, that is an easy choice. But again, people tend to hesitate when these opportunities come around.

There is so much knowledge available to us through the mediums we have discussed so far in this chapter. You really have to take advantage of the ease of access to them because there has never been such a low barrier of entry into a position of power in our lifetime!

Step 7: Preparing For The Worst

There is always a balance between highs and lows in the market. I am no expert, but by looking at the market briefly, we see that we have been in a strong bull market since the 2008 crash. This means this bull market has lasted over ten years. What does this mean? Well, historically, bull markets tend to last six to eight years before a major correction hits, followed by a one to three year bear market. Simply by looking at the charts and trends, we are in a very over extended bull market, and we are seriously due for some sort of major correction or bear market. Again, I have no idea what will actually happen, this is just my opinion. But, markets always do correct themselves, because what goes up must come down. So eventually, shit may get ugly for a little while but that is okay, because if you're reading this, you will be well prepared.

The theme of this chapter is that NOW is the time to invest in yourself. Well, look, it is easier than ever to invest in yourself at the moment I am writing this. I am not sure what will be going on when you get the chance to read this. But either way, we need to take full advantage and ride the bull market wave. Because, again, a bear market will hit sooner or later. Those opportunities on social media that we talked about will be cut in half. Brands won't be able to afford paying people like you and me to manage their social media accounts. Companies will go bankrupt and will go out of business. Shit gets ugly during bear markets, and it won't be a land of opportunity for everyone like we are seeing now.

This is a once in a lifetime situation for a lot of people. There is just so much opportunity, it is truly overwhelming. The last thing you want in your life is regret. Make the right choices so that you don't have any regrets when the bear marker hits and shit goes south.

Step 8: If You Don't, Who Will?

Here is the one thing you need to realize right away. Picture this scenario. You are working on a startup or an idea, and you are seeking funding to further the progress or to continue with the process. You land a few meetings with investors and venture capitalist funds. You prepare your elevator pitch and your pitch deck and it is PERFECTED. You go in there, shake hands, make a killer pitch and then they ask you "So how much have you invested in to this yourself?" and you answer "Little to none of my own money, that is why I am here.".

You will be rejected 11 out of 10 times. I promise you, no matter how good your idea and pitch were, NO investor will invest into your pitch if you haven't invested anything into it yourself. Just think logically for a second. If you are sitting in their seats, what vibe or message do you get when the founder tells you that they haven't put in a relevant amount of their own capital into this project? To me, and to all investors out there, it sends the vibe that the founder or team does NOT believe in what they are selling.

This little example applies to ALL areas of life. Whether you like it or not, you are going to need to sell every single day of your life. Sales is everything. If you don't buy into yourself, or if you don't believe in yourself, then how in the world are you going to get professionals to believe or invest in you? It is utter nonsense!

Before you go out and try to sell yourself, make sure that YOU buy it. You must believe it, you must buy into it. Always ask yourself how you can invest in what you are doing. Take it as far as possible and give everything you can possibly give before you ask outside investors to invest in to what you are doing. Your rejection tally will be noticeably lower.

Step 9: Take Risks NOW

This whole chapter is about one word, and that is NOW. There is so much importance behind that word, especially in business and entrepreneurship. There is a lot of competition out there and this game is not at all easy. Everyday that you wait will make whatever it is you are trying to accomplish that much tougher. It is just true fact. One of the most important parts of being in business for yourself and striving to be financially free is taking risks. Now, that may scare a lot of people away, but it absolutely shouldn't. Taking risks is essential. It isn't just a recommendation, it is absolutely required.

Now, if you are like myself, a student of school, whether it be college or high school or whatever else, than you are in the best situation that you'll ever be in for the remainder of your life. It is so much easier for people like us to take risks. If you are not in this category, and you are decently far along in your career, you have a family, and so on, then it is going to be a lot harder, but it is still very possible. Let me explain.

For the younger generation and the group of upcoming innovators and entrepreneurs, please do me a huge favor and read this chapter over and over again, especially this specific step. The first reason why you need to take risks today is because you do not have your own family to worry about. Family comes with so much responsibility, including time and money. Family is the most important aspect of my life and I can not wait to have my own family. So, this is why I am taking risks now, because I do not yet have a family; meaning I don't need to worry about the negative impacts that the risk I take can have on that family. This is a huge ordeal with so many entrepreneurs and it is very unfortunate. Starting to work on yourself now is so crucial.

I work at a local incubator for a majority of my day. I have a part time sales job with one of the startups there and I am a part of the accelerator program that they offer through the university. There are a handful of companies that rent space at this building and a lot of them are working on some truly amazing things.

I was doing some work for one of those companies, helping them to create content, and one thing stood out when we worked together. The founder was older, which is totally fine, because anyone at any age can do these things. But, what stood out was the added barriers due to the fact that he had a family to take care of. He would often show up to our meetings late, as he was coming from his other job. He couldn't take a risk of letting go of that other job because his entire family relied on that.

This was obviously a big deal for his startup, because as a founder, every minute and every hour matters. If you can't be there with the team because you have to be at another job during the day and so on, it will be that much harder. And again, it is obviously still very possible for these people to succeed, so many have done it under similar circumstances. The point is that it makes it so much harder than it would be right now, when you don't have these responsibilities.

The funny thing is, as I am writing this story, there are dozens of people that come to mind who will 100% think that this story is about them. It is so common! It is just one of those reasons that really stands out. You live one life. The life you dream of it out there and it is reachable. But, risks need to be taken. Not every time will those risks pay off, and that is what you'll need to be prepared for. There are a lot of people out there trying to build amazing things, but most of them aren't willing to do what it takes. If you are willing to take risks, then you will get to where you want to go quicker than any of your competition. Take risks NOW!

My Case Study

Step 1 in this chapter was to explain and to understand the power of NOW. In my own experience, I have the most success when I take immediate action, and this is true for most humans. I have some experience with network marketing and sales, and the number one thing that was stressed was the power of now. There is an incredibly important law of money and success that plays into this, and that is the law of diminishing marginal returns. This is so evident through my experience in these fields. For example, on a cold call with a potential client, there are times when they don't close right on that call. Chances are, each follow up call you do with that prospect, they will be less and less excited and interested in what you were trying to sell them. Same with network marketing. If you show them a presentation and get them amped up about the great things that this gig can do for them but they don't get on board immediately, their excitement and interest will fade away. And lastly, this is true when starting a business on your own. As soon as you have thought of that great idea, you are full of excitement. But if you don't capitalize on that abundance of ENERGY, than you will begin to lose motivation and drive towards making that idea happen. Start now and don't let that momentum slip away!

Step 2 was to be proactive. This is one of my strong suits to be totally honest. A lot of people like to settle, or to stay at the pace of the crowd. For me, I have always been proactive and I always try to think ten steps ahead. Being proactive at a young age may be my biggest blessing. It has brought so many opportunities to the table to succeed in business and entrepreneurship. It also has helped me to connect with some amazing people and set myself up for success in life after college and higher education. Being proactive is not very hard either, it is more about knowing how to be proactive, and I hope you learned a thing or two from that section.

Step 3 was one of the most valuable sections in this book and it was how exactly to invest in yourself. The methods and means of doing so that I mentioned in that section were all tested first hand by myself and truly had a life changing impact on my career thus far. But there is one thing you should know about me as well, and that is I hated reading. I don't think I read an entire book before I turned 16 and that is the cold hard truth. I absolutely despised reading, I just could not do it. But one day, my grandfather, who is one of my closest mentors, gave me a book called *The 22 Immutable Laws of Marketing* by Al Ries and Jack Trout and I was astonished. The information in there was not a history lesson or related to anything I had learned from school at the time, but it was real world case studies from businesses and companies that I admired. Best of all, every piece of advice in that book was easy to understand and apply to real life happenings. From there, I was hooked. But I still don't LOVE to read, and luckily, I don't have to because of the abundance of other means of educating. The ones I mentioned were YouTube and other paid courses. These can all be life changing if you give them a fair chance.

Step 4 was to work for free. To be honest, all the work I have done thus far has been for free because I have never been compensated for the hours I put in. I dedicate double the amount of hours to my podcast, brand, and startups than I do to anything else in my life. I do not expect to be paid, and when I do get some money, I put it all back into the business. I am 100% confident that the money and time I put into these things now will pay me ten fold when I really need it to.

Step 5 was to compare the ROIs of your everyday activities. There are a lot of decisions that you have to make everyday, and a lot of us end up making the wrong ones and are left with the feeling of regret. Like everyone else, I hate that feeling and to prevent it from happening so often, I started to think before acting. Not just think, but think in a specific way. In college especially, this has helped me to optimize time and get done the things that matter most. There will always be temptation and peer pressure, but you'll learn how to fend that off eventually.

Step 6 was explaining why knowledge is power. I can tell you first hand that I have learned so much more from business books that I have read than what I learn from higher education and over ten years in the schooling system. Knowledge is very powerful, but you must seek knowledge because even though it is easily found, it takes effort to actually consume and apply it. Be patient but stay consistent and always be learning.

Step 7 was to prepare for the worst. To be honest, if I read that section a year or two before today, I would have no idea what any of that means. To put it simply, now is a time that we will look back on in the years to come and say "Damn, those were AMAZING times!" There is just so much opportunity out there right now for literally anybody with drive and ambition. Go out there and get it before it is too late!

Step 8 was if you don't invest in yourself than who will? When I was working on my second startup, Your Call, I was preparing a pitch deck for a pitch event in my local area. I had watched a ton of Shark Tank and other pitch events on YouTube and they were very well done. But, I noticed something from my pitch was missing. This was a great idea, but why me? Why would they invest in me to execute on this pitch? I hadn't put much into the idea, as it was just an idea at the time. As you could have predicted, the pitch didn't go very well. So, knowing exactly why, I set out to fix those problems. I invested that entire summer of my junior year in high school to learning iOS design, and by the time summer was over, I had put together 80+ pages of iPhone screen designs for the app I wanted to build. Now, I could go to investors and show them that I was not playing around with this anymore. I was invested into it MYSELF. If you want to be taken seriously, than you have to take yourself seriously first.

Step 9 was to take risks now. I know from my experience of working around tons of different startups and founders that risk taking is a key aspect of every success story. You have to be willing to take risks. I have taken a few risks so far, and a majority of them did not work out. But hey, I am still alive. I am living a great life. I still have food on the table, a great family, and everything else that I could ever need. If I had been 10-20 years older when I took those risks, the results would have had a much more significant impact to my life and those around me at the time. Take risks while you are young! Learn what it is to fail now so that you can set yourself up for future success.

Chapter 7: Finding Your Support Group

—————————————————————————

"Mentors have a way of seeing more of our faults than we would like. It's the only way we grow." - George Lucas

—————————————————————————

Step 1: Entourage

"You are who your friends are." You have probably heard this saying over and over again and it is one of those sayings that actually always holds true. Just a quick shoutout to my own entourage, my ride or die squad: Max Stanton, Dan Crowley, and Mitch Haykal. This is my core entourage.

Your friend group says a whole lot about you and what you do. If you surround yourself with ten drug dealers, than you'll most likely become the eleventh. If you surround yourself with 5 millionaires, than you'll most likely become the 6th. If you surround yourself with a few unmotivated friends, than you too will be unmotivated. Your environment and the people that make up that environment have such a heavy influence on who you are.

In high school, you'll most likely float around a few peer groups. Like we talked about before in this book, you do not need to please everyone. You do not have to be liked by everyone and you certainly do not have to be friends with everyone. That doesn't mean be a dick or show them hate. Always be kind and act with love and empathy. But the biggest problem in high school is, when kids strive to be friends with everyone and to be liked by everyone. Rather than keeping a close knit friend group that they can trust and relate to, they surround themselves with everyone in their sight. They feel the need to be a part of every friend group, every rumor, every conversation, and be invited to every party and so on. For me, this was probably a lot more common given that I went to a private high school and I knew every single kid in my grade. But either way, you have to learn how to narrow down and find your support group, or what I like to call your entourage.

I don't know if you've ever seen the tv show Entourage, but it was one of my absolute favorite shows growing up. I used to watch the show with my own entourage, which consisted of my younger brother and my two cousins. I had a close friend group in school as well. Of course, I was nice to everyone in high school and loved to talk with many people, but I always kept a close knit friend group who I knew would be loyal and loving.

Think of it this way, would you rather have four quarters or ten dimes? This is the way you should think when closing in on your friend group or your entourage. In my opinion, four quarters is a lot better to have than ten dimes. They add up to have the same value, but I would much rather be a part of a more exclusive group. In high school especially, friends are super important to have. There are always going to be tough times, and having a support group of friends and family that you can rely on at all times will be crucial to your well being.

Another thing to know is that this doesn't have to be permanent. I have been really close with some people at a certain point in life and now we don't talk much. This is very common and to be expected. People change and are influenced by outside environments and that is completely fine. You have to learn not to take it personal and to understand that this is how things work sometimes. At some point, you'll need to separate yourself from some friends as well. Always put your well being first, and then ask how you can be of service to others.

Again, environments have such a powerful influence on the type of person you are as well as your everyday actions and habits. By surrounding yourself with a close knit entourage made up of people with like minded goals and thoughts, you are setting yourself up for success.

Step 2: It's Okay To Ask For Help

Not only is it okay to ask for help, but you're most likely going to need to get into the habit of asking for help. There are so many resources out there and so many people who have successfully went through the trials and tribulations of their own entrepreneurship journey, and these people can be super helpful to what you want to accomplish. Funny thing is, they probably learned everything they know from some other entrepreneur that went before them and so on. You just have to accept the fact that you do not know everything. Be open minded, don't be arrogant. Unlike in school or anything else you are used to in life, making mistakes in entrepreneurship can be extremely costly and can have long term effect on your startup. There is literally ALWAYS going to be somebody available to help you out when needed, so take full advantage.

The problem with a lot of entrepreneurs, and I faced this as well when first starting out, was the secrecy aspect behind what they are working on and what not. There has always been this idea going around that you can not share your ideas or what you're working on with anyone because they will just steal it. Well, that is just not true, and to be blatantly honest, ideas are not worth shit. Think about it like this, have you ever seen a successful company or a successful product and think to yourself "Damn, I thought of that idea a long time ago!"? Exactly, we all have had that thought before. That just shows that ideas are absolutely worthless. Thousands of people had the idea for Twitter, it wasn't just Jack Dorsey. So, maybe now are you willing to share your idea so that you can get the help and advice that you'll NEED ?

Next, entrepreneurs are sometimes very arrogant, especially in the very beginning stages. There is this misguided view of entrepreneurs portrayed by Instagram influencers and what-not that give people the idea that being an entrepreneur is super cool and all that. When people see this, they decide to be an entrepreneur (QUICK RANT: Nobody decides to be an entrepreneur, you can call yourself an entrepreneur all you want but if you can't back it up with anything that you have done that was entrepreneurial then it is just a buzzword in your Instagram bio.)

They think now that they are an entrepreneur, they are cool, they are smart, and all that good stuff. This becomes a problem because so often I will see these aspiring entrepreneurs be arrogant towards their peers or elders who could be of great service to them and their startup. Do not be afraid to ask for help! You should be open to ALL opinions and ALL criticism. This is not an easy journey, not at all. It will feel lonely, tiresome, and ruthless. Ask for help! There is always a support group around you that can literally give you that last push towards the finish line or pick you up off your feet.

Another reason why you HAVE to share your ideas and what you are working on is because as the founder, you have a ton of bias. With every decision you make, there will be bias involved. Don't make that mistake! Show a few open minded people and get their feedback, they may help you to see a serious flaw that you would have never seen.

Again, you have to get into the right mindset to execute on this book effectively. It will always come down to the correct mindset. Having the humble and open mindset will help you to seek help when you truly need it, as well as a second opinion when bias may be involved too heavily. We are not supercomputers. We can not do everything on our own. We don't know everything. There is a wealth of knowledge and experience out there, use it.

Step 3: Be Nice To Yourself

Okay, so this step is sort of like a timeout from everything that you've been reading in this book thus far. Mental health and well being are so important and people do not give these things enough attention and thought. Mental health is a real issue, especially in today's society. You may need to take a mental health day or a day off. You may need to take a break from social media. Be nice to yourself! Work hard enough and get enough things done so that you can feel good about yourself and feel deserving when you do decide to take a break.

Every entrepreneur and successful businessman has gone through things like this. Everything that we have discussed so far can be overwhelming, I completely understand that. That is why we covered things like having a strong and proper mindset, having a support group, finding a business partner, setting incremental goals, and so on. Take it one step at a time. There are times when things are going to get extremely stressful and that is okay, we all experience this at some point. Be nice to yourself and take off time, do something really fun, go out and experience nature.

For me, this consists of things like watching my favorite show on Netflix, or going for a run outside, or grabbing dinner with some friends. Make these things your reward at the end of a long day, or at the end of a goal being completed. Everyday before I go to bed, I watch Netflix. Sure, many people are going to say that I am an idiot and I am wasting time and so on. Well, I work my butt off the entire day and I enjoy watching 30 minutes of Netflix before going to bed. Do whatever works for you! As long as you feel that you deserve it, than it can't hurt. Just don't take advantage, be a good coach to yourself. Don't lose sight of the end goal here.

Step 4: How To Get What You Want

So far, we have covered a few different ways to get what you want, as we have talked about things like reaching out to influencers, offering to work for free, trading value and so on. There are a lot of ways to do this and you'll eventually find what works best for your own unique approach and then go with it. But, how exactly do we get what we want? Well, it all starts with one thing, and that is figuring out WHO do we want.

What people do not realize is that no matter how much they love themselves and want to rely on only themselves and so on, literally everything that they could ever desire is in someone else's possession. Someone else will always have what you want. So now it is a question of HOW you are going to get that. Think about it, in every scenario that you have a need or a desire, it is in someone else's possession. When you first develop your product and are ready to sell it, what are you looking for? Customers of course, but what about these people make them good customers? They have money! They have money to exchange for whatever the product is that you are selling. Remember, everything in life is a sale. You have to be able to not only find and identify these people, but you also need to be able to sell to them or make an exchange of value so that you can get what you desire.

You want guidance and you want knowledge. Sure, books are a great place to start, but take it one step further and find a mentor or find a teacher. They have what you want! Now you have to go out and get it from them. This isn't theft or anything, it is just an exchange of value. Your job is to figure out what you have to offer. That is the entire goal of this book. What gifts of real value do you have to offer to others? Once you find that, you are set for life.

Step 5: Be a Giver

Giving is key in every aspect of life. Like Gary Vee says, positivity always wins and you must give and give without expectations of receiving anything. Give out of pure generosity to others. You need to learn to become a giver, and with no strings attached. As soon as you start to give with the expectation of receiving something in return, you lose. If you are always doing something because you think it'll lead to you receiving the benefit later on, than you aren't really giving. That is artificial, and it is not authentic at all.

Entrepreneurship is hard, and you are going to run into a handful of problems and situations. But, you'll learn from them, and then you'll get really really good at doing certain things. Be willing to give those gifts to others who may be struggling. If you are making amazing content and you see a page that is struggling with their content, send them some of your best tips. Or even send them some custom content, you may even get a future customer out of that. Be willing to extend your hand to others because that good deed will pay off for you in the future. You'll feel good about yourself. There is way too much negativity flowing around social media and the entrepreneurship community, we need to flip the switch.

Don't get greedy either. You can receive as well, but only what you deserve. There may be a surplus on the table, but only take what you need. As soon as you begin to take with both hands, you are taking too much. There is more than enough to go around for everyone reading this as long as you are willing to do what it takes. The information in here is quite simple, but it is up to you to execute and make it happen. Always lead with positivity and generosity, it always wins. Always.

Step 6: Mentors

Mentorship is SO important and it will play such a major role in all of the things we discussed so far. We briefly talked about mentors as well as self education in the form of reading, watching, listening, and so on. These are all key to your personal development, but mentors take that to the next level. Finding a mentor will be absolutely essential to your success in whatever field you are in, and we will talk about how to find one, why you need one, and how to get the most out of your mentor.

In this chapter so far, we have talked about friend groups and surrounding yourself with the right people. This all funnels into mentors. Mentors are people who guide you in the right direction. They help you to see your FULL potential that you may have never seen in yourself. They help to hold you accountable to those goals that you set for yourself in the earlier chapters. They help you figure out how to get from point A to point B. More importantly, mentors are people who you want to be like. Someone that has achieved what you'd like to achieve one day. Someone who you can relate to and feel comfortable around.

There is this great debate about true mentors now that you have access to tons of people over the internet. In my opinion, and from my experience, true mentors are people who you can meet with in person every so often. Tons of people will buy coaching calls or online trainings and call those people their mentors even if they have never held a conversation together in person. That is fine because you can still learn plenty from those people, but the most important and real mentors are those who you can call up later today to grab dinner or meet with in person to go over some things. The people online are more like teachers. To you guys, I am more like a teacher rather than a mentor unless we know each other and spend a good amount of time together in person.

I am not discrediting anyone, but I am simply providing insight into what works best in terms of finding mentorship. If you are seeking a mentor, stop trying so hard. Everyone gets so stressed when they hear that they NEED to find a mentor. It isn't a necessity at this very moment. And little do you know, they are right in front of you!

My grandfather and my dad are two of my biggest mentors. My dad being the biggest and most important because we spend time together every single day and work on business together. He has taught me the ins and outs of the business world and mentors me everyday, guiding me to make the best decisions within the companies we work together on.

My other mentor, Roger, who helped me to write this book, was also right in front of me. He is technically family, and I would see him every week. It wasn't until I started my podcast that he became my mentor. But, back to the main point, they are usually the people who are right in front of you. And in some cases, they might not be and that is totally fine. In my own experience, and hearing stories from dozens of other world class entrepreneurs, mentors almost always will find you, as long as you are looking and paying attention. Be patient, the right mentor will come to you eventually.

Virtual mentors are also great to have. Even though the connection and the relationship may not be as genuine and real, they are still necessary to have. Like I said, you will need multiple mentors. They might not all be physical mentors, some of them may be people that you have never met and never will meet. In my own experience and opinion, you at least have to talk to that person for them to be your mentor. Even though I watch hours of his content, I don't think that Gary Vee is my mentor because we have yet to hold a conversation. Even though we will be working together in the future, he just isn't a mentor to me because there is no established connection yet. That doesn't mean I can't spend hours a day consuming his content.

There are online mentors everywhere. They are so accessible. Every mid level influencer on the internet has some opportunity

145

available to you for mentorship, whether it be a coaching program or a mastermind group that they have. It is definitely available if you seek it out.

You may only have one in person mentor and again that is totally fine. There are a ton of ways to define success, but in my opinion, success is achieving greatness in the core areas of your life that matter the most to you. For me, that is family, faith, and business in no particular order. I need a mentor for each of those three categories. How do I become a better family man? How can I contribute more? How can I get better at business and produce more income for my family and for myself? How can I reach and help more customers? How can I build a stronger and more powerful relationship with God? How can I find his purpose for me? How can I pray more effectively everyday? These are all the right questions to be asking. Remember, it is all about the mindset and the quality of the questions you are thinking about. Find those answers through your mentors. This is the fast track to success and fulfillment.

You can also have multiple mentors. Make sure that your mentor is someone who is successful in whatever it is you are trying to accomplish. You can have a mentor for sports, for business, and for faith. Think of it like that, mentors can be specific to certain categories in your life. Once you find out what you need a mentor for, then that is how you find the right mentor. They are everywhere, you just aren't looking hard enough.

Step 7: Hire For The Rest

Remember earlier in this book when we talked about finding your passion and discovering your unique abilities and strengths? If not, definitely go back and check it out. It is so crucial that you are aware of your abilities and what makes YOU great. Business can be made very simple once you figure out what value you can provide to others. Business is simply the exchange of value. If you can provide lasting value consistently and effectively, then people will be willing to exchange money for that value. It is that simple. Business is just facilitating transactions, do not over complicate it.

Okay, so now you found your strong suit in life and say it is that you are an incredible sales person as well as an idea person. Take Sir Richard Branson for example. Branson is one of my absolute favorite entrepreneurs of all time. He is super cool and is ultra successful in his ventures. He is good at what he does, but he is not good at everything else. Wait, what? Who am I to say that about one of the most well accomplished entrepreneurs?

Well, on a previous podcast episode, one of our guests had shared the stage with Richard at various speaking events and they had a lasting friendship. What he pointed out to us was that sure, Richard is an absolute genius at what he does, but he sucks at business in general. He flat out sucks. He barely knows how to keep his finances in check and so on. But, he is a rockstar at being a leader and being an idea man. He is one of the very best at doing that. He is also a rockstar at many other things. So, how does somebody who sucks at business go on to become one of the most repeated successes in business in out entire history? It is because that one other thing that he is

147

an absolute wizard at is hiring other people to do what needs to be done. That is literally it! Richard may not be the best at actually doing the internal things that need to be done inside a business, such as balancing the books and the million other day to day tasks that need to get done, but he is the best at what he does; and that is hiring people to do those things that he is not good at. How genius is that?! That is, in my own experience, the most pure example of what I am trying to teach to you here. You do not have to be good at every single business operation and component. It wouldn't hurt to be, but it is way more valuable to hone in on one of the more important tasks and become the absolute best to ever do that. Not only once, but consistently over time.

Just like you all, I was blown away by this story. I was so excited when I heard it because it confirmed my idea that you are reading about right now. You do NOT need to be good at everything. It is that simple. I realized this from being close to my dad and my grandfather, my two biggest inspirations, due to their great success in business and entrepreneurship.

My grandfather was a business genius. But get this, it is 2019 and he has NEVER accessed the internet. EVER. He is still working for the business that he founded years ago. He has been for his entire life, yet still to this day, he has never sent a text message, email, or anything along those lines. He doesn't need to! He executed on this strategy, and instead he hired people who were good at using the internet. He focused on what HE was good at, and that was similar to the traits of Sir Richard Branson. My dad did essentially the same thing. He was born in Lebanon and immigrated to the United States during the war there. He came here and built one of the best real estate portfolios around. He never did good in school, but he found something that he was great at and passionate about and he capitalized on that. It is that simple!

Step 8: Applying It To School

The main target audience of this book is definitely college and high school students, although the information here can be of extreme value to anyone of any age. I wanted to touch a little on how this chapter and the steps involved apply to school. How do you find a good support group in school? This is a great question. In high school, this is your opportunity to test things and find yourself. Be nice to everyone, but also remember that you don't owe anyone anything. In college, you have a lot of freedom to make a friend group. You won't know 99% of the people on campus and the best part is that you don't have to get to know them if you don't want to.

In my own experience, you should find a great group of friends and stick to that for as long as it lasts. If you did a good job picking this group than it should last a lifetime. But in high school, there is way too much drama and all that bullshit that comes with who's friends with who and all that good stuff. Find that small group of friends and then commit to that.

There is always going to be drama, but you better back off and get as far away from that as possible. It is poison and nothing good ever comes from that. But again, this doesn't mean that you can't be nice to everyone. Be nice, but remember that you don't owe anyone anything. There is a great distinction between being nice to someone and being their friend, or doing deeds for them without reason or logic behind it. Sure, you can be a nice person and do that occasionally, but never put yourself in a situation to be manipulated or taken advantage of.

That brings us back to the idea that some people have in their mind where they think that they have to please everyone. They feel the need to make everyone around them happier and better and so on, and this is with great reason. But it NEVER works. There is never success behind this. All this is going to do is tear you down. You won't last by doing this. It all goes back to the point that I have been trying to emphasize this entire chapter which is that you do not owe anyone anything. Keep that mindset and you'll be free from any of these dangers that I am pointing out. It also all goes back to balance and finding the dichotomy. Not pleasing everyone doesn't mean to be nice to a few people and then be a total jerk to everyone else. Use common sense and make judgements based on that. Finding a dichotomy is one of the most difficult things to do, but it will help you a ton to prevent you from stretching yourself way too thin.

It is a different story in college. At least for me, there are 90% of people on campus that I do not know or recognize. It isn't like high school where everyone is in this small confined box. It is more free and open, and this is absolute freedom. This was the biggest wake up call for me. I didn't know anyone there, and it helped me to remember the reason I was there in the first place, and that was for me to graduate and get my degree. Now I am not saying be selfish, but you have to put yourself first. This is one of the easiest things to do and it is also one of the most important things to do if you want to become happy. And of course, networking is going to be a great opportunity at college but that isn't what we are discussing here; this is more about making friends, not business partners or connections.

You don't need to be friends with everyone. It won't do you any good and it will stretch you too thin. Find a small group back in your early days, people who could be your very own support group. People you can rely on. People that elevate your life and people that you enjoy being around. And most importantly, people who you can be yourself around.

My Case Study

Step 1 in this chapter was to find your entourage. This roots all the way back to a tv show from the early 2000s on HBO. If you haven't seen it, I definitely recommend that you check it out. In short, the show is about a group of four high school best friends who are now all out of school and working on a life for themselves. One of their friends, Vincent Chase, decides to take a gamble on himself by going to Hollywood to pursue a career in acting. His entourage decides to do the same, leaving their lives behind in NYC to help Vincent succeed in his new career. This show taught me a whole lot about life and entrepreneurship. The support group, or his entourage played a huge role in his later success. Him taking a big risk early on also played a major role in his success and the road was not easy. There were some very high and some very low points for Vincent and the entourage. But, having that support group and loyalty to each other paid off in the end. It also goes way back to the best advice I have ever received, which was from my grandfather when he told me that "You are who your friends are." For me, this didn't really hit me until recently, and it is such a powerful and true statement. There is so much truth behind it and once you understand and believe it, it will help you to unlock your full potential and help you to make the right decisions that you want to make.

Step 2 was that it is okay to ask for help. Back in the days, my grandfather would hold contests for all his grandchildren to come up with the best business idea and all that good stuff. The thing that everyone did, including myself, was hide our ideas. Whoever had an idea kept it to themselves. We thought that if anyone heard it or saw it, they would take it. Well, later on we realized that just like us, thousands of other people had that same idea that we had. The difference is out of those 10,427 people that had that same idea, only one of them took action on it right away. This taught me that it doesn't matter what your idea is. Ideas are worthless without action. I learned this at a very young age and now, I rarely let new ideas go to waste without giving them a fair try. So this takes us back to asking for help. Everyone is scared to ask for help because they are paranoid that someone will just take their idea. I thought the same thing, and all that did for me was waste time. Even if 57,284 people have your same idea, you are the only one who can execute it the way you drew it up in your head. It will be unique to you. Just focus on action and execution instead.

Step 3 was to be nice to yourself. Like everyone else, I can be hard on myself at times, some more than others. This is fine, it happens, but it is not a good habit to practice. A lot of people beat themselves up and continue to do this and then when they finally reach success, they are tired, unhappy, lost everyone close to them, and so on. This is a major problem in entrepreneurship, and I am here to tell you to be nice to yourself. I love myself. To be nice to myself, I will allow myself free time with friends, time off for Netflix and so on. If you can't enjoy life in the present than you aren't doing it right. Yes, there will be times when things get hard. But if you are constantly ignoring everything outside of your work, then you are going to lead a miserable life and upset a ton of people, including yourself. I know people hate on movies and tv shows and so on, but I am not giving up my Marvel movies and tv shows. Sorry! Surprisingly, there is a lot to learn from some of these shows and movies. Enjoy them.

Step 4 was how to get what you want. Well really, this is all on the mindset that you have to have. I know we talked a lot about having a small friend group and a tight circle, but that doesn't mean you will cut off your communication with other people. These are the people who have what you want and need. I am still learning this, and I am getting better and better at establishing relationships and communications with the right people. For example, the podcast is great. I don't have to be friends with all of my guests, but I do get their undivided attention for close to an hour. They have the information that I want. Simple as that. Go out and get it.

Step 5 was to be a giver. This is huge for social media especially. You have to give value before asking for something in return. I remember when Gary Vee first said to reach out to 100 or more people you admire. I did that once and never did it again because nobody answered. But when I revisited this strategy for my podcast, I realized why it didn't initially work. It was because I was not providing any value. I was simply trying to take with both hands and give with no hands. This is a losing strategy. Be prepared to give and give before you ask and take.

Step 6 was finding mentors. This has been life changing for me. I have always admired online entrepreneurs and influencers like some of the ones I have mentioned so far. I would read their books, watch their videos and so on. But having a mentor that is local, relatable, accessible and so on is much more powerful. I also feel like a mentor can be someone who is not very far ahead of you, but someone who is constantly moving and improving. That way, you can strive to catch up, and since you are both running towards the same thing, you can even add value to their journey. It is more beneficial to the group as a whole rather than just one end, and I think that is an example of true mentorship. Be patient, work on self awareness and then your mentor and the right people for you will begin to show up. Trust me.

Step 7 was hiring for the rest. This goes back to the solo-preneur ventures that I talked about a while back. I was always the entrepreneur as a kid who would work every aspect of the business. I learned a lot, but I executed poorly on a lot of things because it simply was not my strong suit. Try to find people who can do these things better than you can. These people are employees. They are paid to do what you can't do effectively. You aren't a superhuman. My eyes opened on this subject when I heard that one of my biggest role models, Sir Richard Branson, was just awful at business. You don't have to be good at it all, just get really good at one or a few things.

Step 8 was to apply all of these rules and steps to your college or high school life. For me, I was always the people pleaser in high school, but I realized that it was not doing me any good. It didn't mean that I started to be a mean person, but I started to put myself more often. Everyone usually has their own best interest in mind, so don't put yourself in bad situations where you will be used and manipulated. I found it best to find that entourage and stick with it.

Chapter 8: Opportunities Outside of The Classroom

"The credit belongs to the man who is actually in the arena; whose face is marred with dust and sweat; who strives valiantly, who errs and may fall again and again, because there is no effort without error or shortcoming." – Theodore Roosevelt

---

The Backstory

If you've made it this far into the book, then you are probably well aware of the podcast that I started with my friend from college called Real Talk University: Exploring Success Stories Outside of the Classroom. That podcast and the story behind it is where I got the inspiration for writing this chapter. A major theme of the book is going out and doing more in an effort to find and be the best version of yourself. The podcast plays a major role in helping people to achieve that.

The story behind it is pretty simple. One day, I decided it would be a good idea to start a podcast. I asked a good friend that I met in college if he would be interested in being a host on the show with me. He agreed. That same day we recorded and published our first episode. The end. Pretty straight forward, right? It was simply just taking action towards something we both had an interest in. I would have never forgiven myself if I didn't do exactly that, because that one decision changed my life forever. It opened *my* eyes to what I am trying to open up everyone else's eyes to, the ever flowing amount of opportunities.

Again, going into this, we had absolutely no idea what we were doing. We did not know how to get our voices out of the recording software and on to apps like Apple Podcasts. We simply recorded our first episode and figured it out on the fly. It was the farthest thing from a perfect debut. But I think in today's age, the most important quality and trait of an entrepreneur is to take action. With all the resources to self-educate yourself, it is not hard to learn the basics of putting out a podcast. You can learn as you go, and I assure you that if you put some time and effort into it, it can make a huge positive impact on your life and your career.

Our first few episodes were shaky at best. But we kept grinding, knowing that we had a strong purpose and that many students could benefit from our content if we could get it to where it needed to be. Very soon after, our podcast went viral. We landed on the Apple Podcast charts overnight. We were blown away. We picked up a huge influx of new users and followers on social media and we instantly had more inspiration and stronger motives to continue down this path.

Through the podcast, we have heard some incredible stories from people who have found success in their own unique way and approach. Although the people we interview share similar traits such as persistence, action taking, dreamers, innovators, and more, they are all unique in their own way and it shows in

156

their stories. This has really opened up my eyes to the potential that is out there and the fact that you do not need to do things a specific way. Just be true to yourself and figure it out as you go. It will all work out in the end!

By surrounding ourselves with all of these stories and great minds, we have discovered a ton of opportunities for younger students and college kids to create a side hustle. This chapter will entail a few of the ones that I find to be the easiest to start TODAY, without much money and time. Be sure to test these out and make the most of them, I can guarantee that if you give at least one of these a fair shot, your finances will be way ahead of where you could have ever imagined.

Side Hustle #1: The Reselling Game

Just to clarify before I get into this, I want to point out that these side hustles are not listed in order of the best or worst or anything like that. They are listed in order of what I have had the most experience with. The first side hustle that I would like to discuss is the reselling game. This is simply a business in which you buy a product in attempts to sell it for a higher price to make a profit. It can literally be applied to anything. Any item, any sale, any market, any price. The goal is to resell it quick and make a profit on it. We will analyze these side hustle opportunities by dividing it up into three main categories:

1. Potential
2. Risks
3. How to do it

So as we mentioned for the reselling game, it is simply something that has been around forever. You may have even done this before without noticing. Again, it can be done with any product, as long as you can successfully flip that for a profit. Now, there is a lot to know about this opportunity before you get right into it. The way I started was with limited edition sneakers. It is easier to start or focus on a niche or a product that you love because then you will have a better understanding on the current and potential value. I used to buy limited edition sneakers using computer bot programs for retail prices, and since they would sell out rather quickly, I was able to sell them for a large profit margin. In most cases, they would sell for 2-3x the price I paid for them.

Now, I was only about 15 when I started to really get into this, and I didn't have much money. Truth is, you really do not need much money for this specific niche, especially nowadays there are much cheaper sneaker bot programs and what not. I started with a small loan of $200 from my mom and then simply used my own money to purchase a bot program. I then used my moms investment to buy the sneakers. I successfully got a pair of those sneakers that retailed for a little under $200, and I turned around and sold them for close to $1000. That small investment was worth 5x the price of retail.

Now I was in the clear. I was able to pay my mom back almost immediately, and I was left with close to $800 of cash from that one transaction. Now, opportunities this good probably aren't available anymore, but I still partake in the reselling game to this day. You can still make 2x your money on a ton of different products out there, it doesn't have to be limited to just sneakers. The best part is that you don't need a lot of money, because once you get one item to flip for a good profit, you can just use that profit to buy the next product and that transaction becomes risk free. Then, just rinse and repeat.

The sneaker reselling game definitely took a nosedive since I started a few years ago, but there is definitely still some potential. Another great niche to look at is the tech industry. I have had some success with buying and reselling items such as limited edition game consoles, limited edition game bundles, first drop of the new iPhones, Black Friday deals, and so much more. It works, you just have to get in the trenches and do the work.

This side hustle is definitely more hands on than the others, but the potential is there and the barrier to entry is very minimum. If you are willing to dive deep and stay very attentive to what is going on in specific markets, paying close attention to things like upcoming releases, upcoming special edition products, and so on, then there is a boatload of potential.

The biggest prize here is the effect of starting with a small investment and then compounding that over time. It is great because once you start to make a few successful sales, you will be playing with risk free money that you earned from the previous flips. This is a huge plus as it doesn't require much capital to start and the risk is very minimal.

There are tons of other options outside of tech and sneakers. I have had experience with other things such as limited edition clothing, comic books and so on. But, there is a lot of people who do the garage sale cleanouts. This is simply where you go around to garage sales and you buy things that you think have a lot of value. Gary Vee is famous for doing this recently. People who have done this claim that you can make close to $500 a week, if it is done consistently. This is definitely more intuitive and hands on because you need to travel to different garage sales to find these items.

Another great option, that is basically the same as a garage sale are the apps OfferUp, Craigslist, and even eBay. These are apps that are market places to buy and sell various products. A lot of times, you can find a ton of items that are listed for a price that is way undervalued. On Craigslists, there are a ton of items that are listed for free that can have a ton of value and obviously this is risk free since they are free items that people just want to get rid of. If you spend the time searching for these deals, you will have no problem finding them.

The only risk I have encountered with this is when the product I bought has no resale value, or less than projected. You simply don't lose money, but it can be a pain in the ass to return things and have to ship things back without making a profit.

Side Hustle #2: E-commerce

This is an extremely broad area but we will focus on just a few of the best ways to get in to e-commerce today. E Commerce is a MASSIVE industry, and it continues to grow exponentially year after year. I recently saw a statistic saying that e-commerce is a $220 BILLION dollar market in just the United States alone. It is also growing at close to 20% per year, if not more.

Similar to the resell game side hustle, you will need some money on hand to start your e-commerce side hustle. Depending on what you decide to do or sell, this money will most likely go towards product development and marketing campaigns to sell that product. There are a lot of different side hustles that fall into this category, and it is pretty similar to the resell game except that you take it to the next level and make it your own. In this section, we will discuss how to set up your own online store, what to sell, how to sell, and where to allocate your initial funds for success.

The most well known, notable, and over saturated form of an e-commerce side hustle would have to be drop-shipping. Some of your favorite online retailers have adopted this concept, such as Amazon and Zappos. Drop-shipping first started to catch heat in around 2015, about four or five years ago. For those who are unaware, drop-shipping is a revolutionary concept of starting your own shop online with ZERO inventory on hand. This means that you are not required to make any investment before hand on inventory or product. Simply, when your online store processes a new order for one of your products, your store is typically linked to a supplier who will then send that exact order right to your customer.

You don't have to do any of the work. Everything is done for you. The beauty of drop-shipping is that you are fully optimized as an online store because you are only buying what you have actually sold. The great thing about drop-shipping for people like you and me is that the cost to get started is very low, and the potential is extremely high. It is so efficient because your funds won't be tied up in inventory and stock that might not even sell. That also means you won't have to pay for storage of that inventory. It is a very efficient way to run your online store. Also, once you get started and master the ins and outs of this business, you can essentially have this business of yours running on "autopilot", meaning that all of the work is automated. The only thing that you will need to be very involved in and proactive about is the marketing. We will get to that in just a minute after we analyze the risks of this side hustle.

Now, there are definitely a few negatives and risks here as well. Although it is a very low barrier to entry for so many people like us, this is probably the downfall as well. It is well oversaturated at this point in 2019, or whenever you get around to reading this. There are too many people doing the same exact thing. Too many people are starting dumb e-commerce stores selling dog toys or fidget spinners or whatever it is that is trending. It is crazy! Although there is a lot of competition and a lot of people doing the same exact thing, there is always room to grow and more to bite off if you can do it the right way. There are always smaller, untapped markets or products that you can dominate and make a pretty penny off of. You just have to be smart and strategic with this while also testing out a few different products to sell and marketing strategies.

The only risk here is losing time and a small amount of money. The money you'd lose by starting and failing a drop-shipping store would be insignificant, but the time might not be depending on how far in you got with it. There are obviously tons of other options out there to make a side hustle and do well with it, so trying this and failing after a decent amount of time can be super frustrating. But hey, that is business and this is what to expect. Failure and false starts are what makes us who we are.

If after reading the potential and the risks associated with drop-shipping, here is how I would go about doing this today. I have some experience with this but as I mentioned, it is pretty oversaturated and I was late to the party so I have my attention on other things at the moment.

The first thing to do would be to open an online store on Shopify. If you have never heard of Shopify, check it out and make an account. This is the most well known online store builder, payment processor, and web hosting tool that is out there. I believe that the starting package is $30 a month, and that will get you everything you'll need to get started. They have tons of templates and drag-and-drop features to build

162

a super high level e-commerce store for your drop-shipping business. If you are not very good with technology or website building and do not have time to learn on your own, then you can hire someone for cheap on a website called Fiverr or even Upwork.

The next thing I would do is set up a PayPal business account or a Stripe account. It may be a good idea to get an LLC, which is a limited liability company. This is basically the documentation that will establish your website or business as a real, legally recognized and registered company in whichever state you choose. This will cost a few hundred dollars, so make sure you look into it more and decide if it is necessary for what you are doing. I always like to be safe. Check out LegalZoom and you can get that set up with a very quick turnaround.

Now that you have all of the logistics figured out, you can now focus on what you will actually be selling. What kind of e-commerce store is this? What will the theme be? Will you only sell one type of product or various types of products for the same niche? I recommend you do some research on this. First, I would recommend that you find a niche that interests you and focus solely on that. If you absolutely love pets, then pick your niche as pet products. Your drop-shipping site can include pet food, pet toys, and all of that good stuff. There are tons of resources online to see what is trending in these different niches. Like I mentioned, since drop-shipping is so oversaturated, there are probably thousands of people already doing that. So, check out some of the top performing sites to get an idea of what you should be doing.

As you can see, the most important thing here is research. You'll need to be very aware of what product you are selling and the trends in your niche or market. But once you are confident enough in what you plan to do, you will be good to go from there. So far, everything I have told you to do may have taken you 30-60 minutes, depending on if you have built the website yet. You are essentially ready at this point. In Shopify, you'll have to make sure your account is set up and your website is ready to go live with a domain name and payment integration. They will guide you through these things when you get to them.

See, it doesn't take much to make this happen, you just need to try it for yourself. The most important thing from here on out will be marketing. Make social media pages for your drop-shipping site and begin to run paid Facebook advertisements with your products. Social media marketing will be absolutely vital for your success in this, so be sure to spend time mastering it or pay to have someone do it for you. If you spend funds to have someone do it for you, that is exactly the side hustle that we will discuss next.

Side Hustle #3: Social Media Marketing Agency

At the time I am writing this section, this side hustle is HOT! There is a ton of buzz going around about starting your own SMMA, or social media marketing agency. This concept has been around for a few years, but it has never been as popular and trendy as it currently is. Now, I can't say if that is a good or bad thing. If you are looking to get started, then there are way more resources and it is a lot easier to get started than it was a few years ago. But, there is also more competition and more people that will be able to do that exact same thing.

I just recently launched my own social media marketing agency in my local town, Binghamton, New York. The results have been great thus far. I am getting a high amount of interest and have been working with some clients already, only a few weeks into setting up the company. This is with little to no money down. All that I had spent money on was some courses to learn the process (I recommend Tai Lopez's course) as well as setting up my LLC and building my website. After those small fees, it is almost 100% profit margins. There are a few more risks and potentials that I want to cover before I explain what exactly SMMA is and how you can get started as well.

The potential is definitely there. Some of the biggest influencers and successful entrepreneurs have had tremendous success doing this. It really has no cost and the time barrier is minimal as well. It is 100% recommended that you are very educated on the topic before going out to get clients, so be sure to invest your own time into that if you want to be successful. The potential to make six figures alone from doing this is very evident, and it'd require little effort and work. Most of the courses teach you to outsource your work anyways, although I don't recommend that you do that.

Some other risks of doing this include burning bridges with clients, failure to deliver results which can hinder your name, brand, and overall reputation. This can be especially bad if you are doing this in your local area. Other risks include wasting valuable time, money, and effort into a failed idea. But, this really can work for anyone.

So, what exactly is this side hustle anyways? Well, building a social media marketing agency is exactly how it sounds. You will create a company, most likely using the LLC format, where you'll provide services to businesses to help them with their social media accounts. Quite simply, people will pay you to manage their Instagram, Facebook, and so on. There are a million different ways to structure this and approach it, so I highly recommend you buy a course online because that will show you some of the best ways to do this, especially if you are new to this. Don't be cheap, a $300 course to learn this business is dirt cheap, with the potential to make six figures on autopilot being highly likely and achievable for really anyone.

Another great thing is that you don't need any prior experience. If you suck at social media, no worries, so does everyone else. But by using these courses, you can learn and develop these new skills over the next few months. This startup process will take longer than some of the other options out there, but if you can see yourself working with local businesses, helping them to grow through the use of social media channels. Then, I recommend you check out this glowing opportunity. Again, opportunities like these do not last forever, and you will regret it if you choose to let it pass along. All the tools and resources that you need are online, so get to work. I hope you are able to achieve success in this side hustle!

Side Hustle #4: Why You Need To Start a Podcast

If you have come this far in reading the book, than you probably understand that a lot of my success and connections have come from starting a podcast. This is a true side hustle. It takes a lot of effort, continuously, to make a quality podcast every single week. It cost money for sure. The returns will be minimal in the beginning. But it is far more valuable than any of the other side hustles previously mentioned in this book. Why? Simple. The connections. So far, after about five months into our podcast journey, we have probably spent a few thousand dollars on things like equipment, promotion, hosting, and other things.

We haven't made any of that money back so far, although that doesn't really seem to be the case. The value, connections, and relationships established so far on our journey have paid us back ten fold. Having the emails and cell phone numbers of some of my biggest inspirations and influences is truly amazing. Being able to sit down with these people for a good hour is far more valuable than money. I mean, think about it, a lot of the people we interview sell coaching or consulting programs that value their time anywhere from $100-10,000 an hour! SO yeah, after 30 interviews (so far) with these types of people, the investment has been worth it.

Not only that, but the money is coming. We have products in development. We have courses in development. We have partnerships and advertisements deals in development. These are all going to help us sustain the process so that we can do this for a living and continue to provide immense value to our listeners and ourselves as well. Because we have worked our asses off in the beginning to build a strong foundation, we will be rewarded in the long run. The podcast will bring us seven figures a year in the near future, and it will continue to provide us with these opportunities to connect with world class individuals.

See what I did there? That is called manifestation. I am writing down the goals and the dreams, confidently stating that they WILL happen. Boom! Come back to me in a year and see how effective that strategy is. Here is an article I wrote for Thrive Global, Arianna Huffington's new media company on January 16th, 2019 called "Why You Need To Start a Podcast":

> As we all know, the way content is being created and shared has completely changed over the last few years, and this change has had a huge impact on the world

of business and entrepreneurship. Podcasting is one of these new mediums that entrepreneurs are using to market their authentic self and establish credibility in the business world. It allows you to spread your message, your passions, your identity, and your opinions in unique ways with your targeted niche audience.

Because podcasting is becoming so mainstream, there has never been a better time to get started, and I truly believe that every college student should launch their own podcast. My college best friend and I started a podcast called Real Talk University: Exploring Success Stories Outside of the Classroom a few months into our first semester at college after we both came to a similar realization about the students around us. A majority of them were unaware of opportunities outside of the classroom to create wealth through financial education and monetizing their true passions. We envisioned a podcast where we would interview entrepreneurs who have successfully pursued their passion by taking a path outside of the classroom. The goal of our podcast was to inspire our listeners to find and pursue their passions.

Going into this, we had absolutely no idea what we were doing. But after two short months, we have been able to put out one episode per week while also having the opportunity to interview huge names in the business world that I myself have personally studied and learned from for years prior. For example, I would have never had the opportunity to write for Thrive Global if it wasn't for my podcast. Arianna Huffington suggested that we share the inspiration and ideas we had behind the project. I never would have thought I'd have the chance to not *only interview Arianna but to also write for her!*

Again, going into this, we had absolutely no idea what we were doing. We did not know how to get our voices out of the recording software and on to apps like Apple Podcasts. We simply recorded our first episode and figured it out on the fly. It was the farthest thing from a perfect debut. But I think in today's age, the most important quality and trait of an entrepreneur is to take action. With all the resources to self-educate yourself, it is not hard to learn the basics of putting out a podcast. You can learn as you go, and I assure you that if you put some time and effort into it, it can make a huge positive impact on your life and your career.

Our first few episodes were shaky at best. But we kept grinding, knowing that we had a strong purpose and that many students could benefit from our content if we could get it to where it needed to be. Very soon after, our podcast went viral. We landed on the Apple Podcast charts overnight. We were blown away. We picked up a huge influx of new users and followers on social media and we instantly had more inspiration and stronger motives to continue down this path.

At the time I am writing this article, we have put out 15 episodes of our podcast, which have been listened to thousands of times. We have interviews lined up with big name after big name, all while being paid from things like ads and merchandise! So, why should you start your own podcast? By starting your own podcast, you are creating the opportunity for yourself to be extremely credible and relevant in whatever area of work or passion you are into. Podcasting also gives you a platform to share your voice and your message. So, what is your excuse? I know for sure that everyone in college can do what Christian and I are doing. All it takes is passion and commitment. And of course, taking massive action.

Now, that was written almost three months ago! It is absolutely incredible, the things that we have been able to accomplish in that short time frame once again. And I know, looking back at this in three more months will be even more amazing. Now, you are probably wondering how you can start as well. How can you do this? It really is simple.

There are ways to start a podcast this second, for free without any equipment or money etc. My recommendation is that you use the app/website called Anchor.fm. It is a platform that hosts podcast shows and also allows you to record episodes right in the app. Better yet, it is completely free to use. Many people were skeptical at first about the app, most likely because it is free, but they were just recently bought out by Spotify, one of the biggest media companies out there nowadays. Once you have that app, you are good to go.

Obviously, there are minute steps to take such as making a show title name, description, and so on. These are definitely important, but aren't appropriate for this book. If you are interested in learning the details and being mentored and guided throughout the entire process of you starting your own successful interview based podcast like Christian and I have done, then reach out to us on social media. We offer 1-on-1 mentorship programs where we literally hold your hand throughout the entire process to get you started and launched successfully. You'll be interviewing your biggest inspirations and role models in no time!

Now, back to the book. Again, the Anchor app will be your best friend. There are so many variables to starting a podcast, but if you don't know what you want to talk about, I recommend finding a friend of yours, sit down with them, and speak into the Anchor app for an hour. There you go, episode one. Put it out there and then keep going. Consistency is KEY to this. So, podcasting is definitely a side hustle that is unlike everything else. But the opportunity is so unique in today's age, I just had to put it out there for you all. The process can be very tricky, so be sure to reach out to me with any questions or interest in our mentorship programs!

Side Hustle #5: Trading & Investing

Trading and investing are two of my favorite things to do, but unfortunately, it is the hardest side hustle for most people due to the high risks and high costs. Unlike the other opportunities that I had mentioned thus far, trading and investing is not something you can just start and then learn as you go. You obviously can do it this way, but I can almost guarantee that you'll lose all of your money. There is a steep learning curve for this side hustle, but once you nail it down with a repeatable strategy and so on, it is highly profitable and rewarding with little amounts of work to follow.

Now, what exactly is trading and investing? By this, I mean trading and investing currencies, stocks, commodities and other things in the world markets. The most well known would be the stock market, but it is good to note that there are equal or greater opportunities in markets such as Forex (Foreign Exchange Market), cryptocurrency (Bitcoin, Ethereum, Ripple, etc) and commodity markets like natural oil and so on. There is a ton of opportunity. I see the most failure when new or beginner traders try to focus/learn every one of these markets. The key to trading and investing successfully is to get very very defined and specific. For example, I like to target the stock market but I go even more defined by targeting the technology sector in the stock market. I also diversify my portfolio with other investments in markets that are similar, just be sure to know what you are getting into! That is the most important thing you'll need to know to succeed in this field. KNOW YOUR SH*T!

Now, how exactly do you trade and invest WHEN you are ready? There are tons of resources out there that you can use, and it is best to choose based on personal preference since they are almost all the same. Also, make sure that you are 18 years or older. Investing and trading are both TAXABLE, meaning that if you do either of these things, you are expected to report real numbers and results for tax purposes. You must be 18 to do this, and since you'll need to report it to the government, make sure you are 18 or older. The most common platforms to invest would be Robinhood, TD Ameritrade, Coinbase, and more. There are tons of brokers for your different needs, depending on your investing style as well as your niche. I recommend that as you are learning, you open what is called a demo account. This is an account that allows you to perform actions as if you were live with a real account, but using fake virtual money. It is a safe and secure way to practice and implement the strategies you'll be learning.

There are tons of places to get education for trading and investing. I recommend that you get the most basic education first, learning about all the markets, how they work, and what they do, etc. It is super important to understand the ins and outs, otherwise you will simply be blindly investing which is gambling. After you have a good understanding of how everything works, start to narrow in on your niche. How do you find your niche? Simple, just explore your interests and what you know most about. For me, I chose technology and cryptocurrency because I have always loved technology and innovation. Boom, simple as that. You can always change your niche as well if you aren't having the success you wished for.

Great places to get your education from are places like Google and YouTube. It really is there for you. It always is, you just have to look for it. There are thousands of educational videos to help you. Another option that people choose are to buy personal mentorship or courses from other successful traders that they admire or look up to. Some great people to check out for this are people like Tim Sykes, James Altucher, Jordan Belfort, and so on. They are all very successful in their respective market niches so learning what they do and how they got to where they are can be a game changer for you.

Now, like we mentioned before, this is probably going to be the least attractive side hustle for many of you. It requires a decent amount of funding, involves very high risk, and it has a steep learning curve. Not only that, but I also think the returns are very slow and gradual over time. This is higher level stuff. A good idea if you are short on funding or time, would be to crush it with one of the other side hustles and then funnel that money/profit into a long term investment strategy. That is the goal, for your money to always be working for YOU!

The risks involved are heavy because the markets are so flooded with huge traders and hedge funds that are making daily moves to shift the scope of the markets. These big players, sometimes called whales, can crush a small trader in seconds.

George Soros is probably the most well known whale, and he has the ability to shift world markets at will. And he has done it before in the Forex scene.

The last qualities that you'll need to succeed and perfect is controlling your emotions, which connects to risk management as well. These are essential to your success, so you must take the time to practice them. When traders get emotional, or trade upon emotions, they lose. It is proven over and over again. Your risk management control is super important because if you are not using risk management properly, you will again get crushed by people who are.

If you want to understand how all of this works in one simple quote by one of the most successful investors of all time, Warren Buffett, then here you go: "The stock market is a device for transferring money from the impatient to the patient." Now go out there and educate yourself and make that bread!

Side Hustle #6: Sales Job

Many would not consider this a side hustle, but why the hell not? Let me make my case here. Remember, the ordering of the side hustles I have mentioned in this chapter are not in order of best to worst. In all honesty I think this side hustle, sales, is the MOST important one to have under your belt. Why? Because I believe when starting out, or doing something on the side, you should work to LEARN, not to EARN. I learned this from Robert Kiyosaki in his book, *Rich Dad Poor Dad*, and it has changed my life ever since. This is the MINDSET that you need to shift to when job hunting or looking for a side gig. Evaluate your options based on what you will LEARN rather than EARN.

So, how exactly has this helped me personally? I have had

many part time jobs and side gigs, I have a lot of work experience for a 19 year old. When I first started working, it was at my family company, Save Around, which is a local business that serves the entire country with their coupon books. Great company, great people, and so on, but my role was something that ANYONE could do. I wasn't learning what I wanted to about the business or about the everyday operations of those who were running it, I was simply a cog in the machine. That is totally fine, but I personally was not benefiting from it and after some time, I left. I took a break from working a real job as I tried a few ventures of my own.

I still needed more experience, and to develop new skill sets, the ones that I was lacking. I wasn't generating any income, and things with my own ventures got tougher and tougher. I wasn't being proactive in my search for the next opportunity, and I missed out on a key sign. Luckily for me, this sign presented itself to me another time, and this time, I took action.

Here is a little background to that story. So, the company I work at now is called Bandalier. I have never heard of it and neither had anyone I talked to about it. At a local business summit event, I was pitching one of my companies at the pitch competition in front of investors. As I was preparing, the local businesses were all in the building, making connections with the locals interested in business like myself. Someone named Matt gave me his business card, telling me that he was hiring new talent. I didn't think much of it, because I was mainly focused on preparing for my big pitch that day. Also, the business card only had his name and their website, but the website didn't make much sense to me at the time.

Then, a few weeks later, I was at another local business event for high school students, pitching the same business plan as I was from a few weeks prior. Ironically, one of the judges for the event was Matt from Bandalier. I briefly remember who he was, still not too sure of what exactly his company did. The pitch event went great, and I was voted as the winner for my section. After the awards, there was a speaker to tell us about himself and his entrepreneurial journey. His name was Jeremey, and I related heavily to the things he covered in his speech. Funny enough, he was the CEO of Banadlier, and he was there with Matt who was the manager of the company.

After the speech, I was approached by him and Matt, asking if I was interested in a job in the sales field. NOW I knew what Bandalier was after Jeremey's presentation, and I was intrigued. This was the opportunity that I needed. I knew that I needed a gig where I could learn a new skill set and challenge myself to get uncomfortable and so on. I did some more research and sent in my application a day later. After some interviews, I was notified that they'd like to hire me to be a part time Associate Sales Rep. I knew that I had to take the job, even though I didn't fully want to.

This was one of the best decisions I have ever made. Prior to working there, I had ZERO experience with sales. That is not acceptable for someone who was launching their own companies and products. I was ALWAYS shy speaking on the phone, and hated talking to strangers. This job forced me to be uncomfortable, which is exactly what you should be searching for. The environment is also great because it is a startup. When I joined the company, they were just celebrating their one year anniversary. This is where I needed to be, in a real startup scene. The pay was great too, it was minimum wage with commissions, even for part time reps! But again, that didn't matter, because I was there to GROW and to LEARN, not to EARN. After close to a year working with the team at Bandalier, I have experienced a complete change in my own identity. It has been revealed to me that sales is EVERYTHING. You will always be selling, whether it be a product, your time, or even yourself. Everything is your life is a sale, or a transaction, and before working at Bandelier, I never realized this.

If you want to be successful with the other five side hustles that we have gone over so far, than you will need to be sharp with your sales skill set. It is the MOST important skill you can have. Sales is EVERYTHING. Not just simply getting on the phone and making calls, but in every way and every part of the process. There is so much to learn! My best advice to you is to learn through experience. Sales is tough, and you WILL struggle when you first start out. Even Grant Cardone, my biggest sales mentor, hated and sucked at sales when he first started and now he is the best in the world. Just go out there and put yourself in those uncomfortable situations, as this is the key to building the foundation for your future goals that are much much bigger.

Final Thoughts

"The way to get started is to quit talking and begin doing." - Walt Disney

---

First of all, if you're reading this and you really made it to the end, you're a real one! Seriously, thank you SO much! It means the world to me that you stuck with it and read my book all the way through. If one person made it this far, then all of the work that I put into this book was well worth it.

Now, I am writing this section a few months after I had completed the manuscript. I have to say, I have learned so much over these past few months that I could have easily added to this book. But, that just goes to show the true power and potential of self education. There is no limit on what you can achieve. The information is out there, and you should now have a strong foundation to build upon after reading this book. But, what do you do with the information? How do you *really* find success? Simple. I am blatantly stealing this from Think & Grow Rich, only because I know it to be true and there is no better way to explain it. Desire backed by faith. Read it again. Desire backed by faith. As long as you have a strong desire that is backed by true faith that you will attain what you desire, then you will do exactly that! But wait...

There is MORE to be added. Desire backed by faith...backed by ACTION! That is the true success formula. You have the information. But how will you apply it? There is nothing more important than taking immediate massive action. I believe in you ALL. I truly do, otherwise, I wouldn't have written this book. You CAN do it! It all starts with YOU. Together, we can build a better future.

About the Author

Andre Haykal Jr is a 19-year-old student at SUNY Binghamton University School of Management.

Andre is very proactive and passionate about opportunities OUTSIDE of the classroom. He is also the founder and co-host of a top 100 business podcast called Real Talk University, where he strives to educate a college-based audience about such opportunities.

Andre considers himself to always be a student because no matter how successful he becomes, he believes that there will always be a way to improve or gain more knowledge through self-education.

Andre hopes that his work and his message can inspire the next generation of thinkers, educators, and innovators. God bless!

Be sure to contact Andre for 1-on-1 coaching, mentorship, or guidance. He would love to hear from his fans and readers, so do not hesitate to reach out via email at ahaykal1@binghamton.edu.

You can connect with me on:
🌐 https://www.xpandurbrandagency.com
🔗 https://www.linkedin.com/in/andre-haykal-jr-3117b0133
🔗 https://www.instagram.com/andrehaykaljr

Subscribe to my newsletter:
✉ https://www.wtwtybook.com/vip

Made in the USA
Monee, IL
18 May 2021

68959741R00121